Family
ALL AGE WORSHIP

Family
ALL AGE WORSHIP

NICK & CLAIRE PAGE

Authentic

MILTON KEYNES ● COLORADO SPRINGS ● HYDERABAD

First published 2007 by Authentic Media
9 Holdom Avenue, Bletchley, Milton Keynes, Bucks, MK1 1QR, UK

1820 Jet Stream Drive, Colorado Springs, CO 80921, USA

OM Authentic Media, Medchal Road, Jeedimetla Village,
Secunderabad 500 055, A.P., India

www.authenticmedia.co.uk

Authentic Media is a division of IBS-STL U.K., limited by guarantee, with its Registered Office at Kingstown Broadway,
Carlisle, Cumbria CA3 0HA. Registered in England & Wales No. 1216232. Registered charity 270162

British Library Cataloguing in Publication Data

A catalogue record for this book is available from the British Library

ISBN-13: 978-1-85078-768-6

ISBN-10: 1-85078-768-9

Book Design by Nick Page

Cover Design by fourninezero design.

Print Management by Adare

Printed and bound in Great Britain by J. Haynes & Co., Sparkford.

Contents

READ THIS FIRST

This is the second book in a series of resources for All Age Worship.

In this book we are exploring the joys and pains of family life, both in our nuclear families and in our wider church family. While individual relationships and experiences differ hugely, everyone, at some point, has had a mother and a father. And most of us have a wider family as well: sisters or brothers, sons or daughters, aunts, uncles, cousins, and second-cousins twice removed called Boris. These relationships can be a source of great love, care and support; they can also be a right pain.

So the aim of these services is to help families. In an age where family life is under threat, we think it's really important that the church does all it can to help people live together in ways which are positive and loving, and where we can keep the shouting down to a minimum.

Style

As in the first book, the emphasis in this book is on action, discussion and entertainment. These services, exploring different aspects of family life, involve movement and activity, listening and watching, problem-solving and reflection. Once again, we design the services for whole-service teaching, with each part of the service intended to move the teaching forward.

Following the script

A lot of the book is in a script format, which doesn't mean you have to be able to act! Although some parts are obviously dramatic, most of the time it is no different to scripted liturgy.

Using the ideas

You can use this book in the following ways:

▷ Do the services exactly as they are presented, from beginning to end.

▷ Pick which bits of the services work for you and use those.

▷ Nick the ideas and adapt them to your own ends!

Know your audience

One of the most important factors in the success of All-Age services – or, indeed, any communication – is to know your audience. If you have a good relationship with the people in your congregation and know them well enough, you will be able to adapt the programme to suit your particular circumstances. So look carefully at the distribution of ages, the gender mix and the ability spectrum. In particular it's helpful to think about:

▷ people who are deaf or who have partial hearing

▷ the blind or partially sighted

▷ those with restricted mobility

▷ anyone with cognitive learning difficulties (mild, moderate or profound)

Overview

The first two pages give an overview of the service, showing the overall aim and how the whole thing fits together. Each service is split into four parts:

1. Want it!

This is where you introduce the subject matter and get people interested in learning. To teach people properly, you have to make them curious and interested enough to learn. Ice-breakers set the tone of the service; the introduction is a promise of what they're going to get.

2. Watch it!

This is the place for the Bible readings or sketches or presentations. Although people watch this bit, they don't sit still. Discussions, treasure hunts, acting scenes out; there's a lot of moving around and discovery.

3. Try it!

This is where they learn for themselves: reflecting, praying, solving problems. The golden rule of teaching is: don't spoon feed your students. Teach them what they need to know, then get out the way as quick as you can!

4. Live it!

This is where you help people to take the learning forward into the coming week: something to take away as a reminder or as a stimulus to action, or a challenge to face up to – applying Sunday teaching to Monday-to-Friday lives.

Running order

This is a simple grid which can be photocopied, listing the elements of the service. You can add in your own details, such as hymns/songs, notices, timings, etc. You can fill in the initials of whoever is responsible for any of this.

Resources

The next few pages give the actual resources for the service: games, drama, discussions, prayers and more. These are grouped under the **Want it! Watch it! Try it! Live it!** headings.

Stand up and listen

This provides a way in to the subject of the service and makes sure the focus is clearly on God. We've adapted Bible verses and put them together to give a flavour of how God is described in the Bible. If you prefer to use the actual verses themselves, the references are given so that you can do that.

Talks

We have kept the direct talk to the congregation to a minimum. It's a sermon-free zone. There are sections for 'the Leader' to say. You are, of course, free to add in whatever you like; you can simply put the main points in your own words, or you can say something else entirely!

Discussion

Ensure the questions are clear and that there is enough time for people to have a go. Get feedback whenever possible – but vary the ways you do it. And keep it short.

 ▷ Questions in these boxes are discussion points. This is where you get the congregation to do some of the work.

Creating groups

Every service makes use of group work. Sometimes it's best – as is suggested by PairTalk – simply to turn to the person nearby. When larger groups are called for, you can try different ways of creating a mix of people, such as grouping people according to which month they were born in, what their first name or surname begins with, height order, or simply numbering them off, if the congregation isn't too numerous. Not everybody wants to be coerced into group work, so it takes a bit of tact and charm to persuade people. But it's worth the effort!

TakeAway

This is something for the participants to take away with them from the service, to remind them of something they've decided to do.

Improvisation

There's a lot of drama in these services, most of it scripted. Sometimes there is room for improvisation. One approach we've used which requires the use of improvisation is called 'hotseating'.

'Hotseating' is not what happens when your electric blanket goes wrong. It means putting the characters you've seen in the drama into the 'hotseat' where they have to answer questions, defend their actions and respond to people's ideas.

The actors, therefore, have to improvise answers in character, imagining what their character would say or do in response to the audience's questions. This is not as difficult as it sounds because, within certain limits, the actor is free to say what they like. All they need is a bit of imagination.

There are no right answers or scripted lines. The purpose of this is to get the audience applying and articulating their knowledge of the Bible in relation to an imaginary scenario. Then when a similar real life situation comes along they know what to do or say.

The important thing is to have good questions – questions that help the congregation to understand why the characters behaved as they did. So avoid questions that require just 'Yes' or 'No' answers.

Naturally, the audience will make up their own questions, but you will probably want to have a few questions up your sleeve. It's worth showing these questions to the actors so that they think through the possible answers beforehand. They need to answer in a way that seems consistent with their character.

Recurring characters

Gordon the Gargoyle

Gordon the Gargoyle helps us apply what we've learned. We attend an Anglican Church where, high up inside the building, there are a number of carved stone heads. One of those became Gordon, who has been in the church for centuries and seen it all. Gordon was voiced by Nick (hiding in a side room with a microphone). Of course your church might not have gargoyles, internal or otherwise. You have a number of choices here.

▷ Build your own gargoyle and tell people you thought that all churches should have one.

▷ Turn Gordon into another character. There are a lot of puns using rock, stone, etc. so he could be a statue, or some part of the building. He could simply be a rock, called Rocky. Or Barney the Brick.

▷ You could use a puppet – perhaps a kind of grandfather character. Just use the scripts and adapt them to your purpose.

The first time you introduce Gordon you can use the introductory script on p.125.

The Shaw Family

Sean, Sheila, Sherrill and Shane Shaw help us explore some of the dilemmas facing families today. Shane and Sheila are the father and mother trying to bring up Sherrill, their teenage daughter, and Shane, her brother.

▷ Sean is a loving but frequently baffled and angry father. He tries to understand his children, but they keep making a mess and waking him up.

▷ Sheila is the mum. She has fond memories of when Sherrill had ringlets and Shane still played with his Action Man. She has never quite got over the fact that they have changed a bit.

▷ Sherrill believes that when the world isn't revolving around her, it is totally against her. She is frequently stroppy or, as she would term it, 'misunderstood.'

▷ Shane is a Christian. But that tends to make life more difficult for him, as he keeps on having to forgive everyone. And, he can't understand why they find it so hard to forgive him.

Daisy Daytime

Daisy Daytime is our daytime TV show host. This is where most of the 'hot-seating' occurs *(see above)*. Daisy is a kind of cross between Jerry Springer and Trisha. We could have called her Trisha Springer. But we didn't. Anyway, her job is to quiz the characters, look scandalized, whoop the audience into a frenzy and end each show with a completely inappropriate platitude.

Extras

Getting ready

Here you'll find a checklist of jobs that need to be done during the week before, or on the morning of the service.

Might come in handy

Some services have this section, which contains some interesting facts or background material that you can use in your talks or links, should you wish.

Brothers, sisters and other common household pests

1. BROTHERS, SISTERS, AND OTHER COMMON HOUSEHOLD PESTS

Aim: to encourage good relationships between siblings
Bible: Psalm 133; Genesis 37

1. Want it!

The purpose here is to
▷ contrast the biblical ideal with the reality

We do this by asking people to
▷ listen to the Bible reading
▷ watch the drama of Shane and Sherrill
▷ talk in pairs about siblings and make badges

The tools we use are
▷ Bible: Psalm 133
▷ Drama: you've got to share!
▷ PairTalk: brothers and sisters

2. Watch it!

The purpose here is to
▷ identify some of the problems between siblings

We do this by asking people to
▷ test their knowledge of Bible siblings
▷ watch the story of Joseph and his brothers
▷ listen to Gordon

The tools we use are
▷ Game: sibling quizzing
▷ Drama: Joseph and his brothers
▷ Drama: Gordon's siblings

3. Try it!

The purpose here is to
▷ help siblings to see each other's point of view

We do this by asking people to
▷ hotseat Joseph's family
▷ give them advice

The tools we use are
▷ Comment: sibling rivalry
▷ Daisy Daytime: Help! My son's been eaten by a goat!

4. Live it!

The purpose here is to
▷ plan how to help siblings to get along
▷ pray for good attitudes and relationships

We do this by asking people to
▷ share good ideas
▷ write down what they are going to share
▷ pray for siblings

The tools we use are
▷ TakeAway: a timeshare card
▷ Prayer: for families in need
▷ Closing prayer

Running order

When	What	Who
	Want it!	
	Arrival: handout quiz sheets	
	Bible: Psalm 133	
	Drama: you've got to share	
	PairTalk: brothers and sisters	
	Watch it!	
	Game: sibling quizzing	
	Drama: Joseph and his brothers	
	Drama: Gordon's siblings	
	Try it!	
	Comment: sibling rivalry	
	Daisy Daytime: Help! My son's been eaten by a goat!	
	Live it!	
	TakeAway: a timeshare card	
	Prayer: for families in need	
	Closing prayer	

Want it!

As people arrive, give out the Sibling Quizzing sheets (see p.27) to give them time to look at the questions before the service starts.

LEADER: Welcome to today's service which is all about brothers, sisters, and other common household pests! Later on we'll be doing some sibling quizzing, which means we'll be testing your knowledge of brothers and sisters in the Bible, but let's start a little closer to home.

Do you have brothers or sisters? Do you get on well with each other?

If you have brothers and sisters, it's possible that this relationship will last a very long time, maybe longer than any other relationship. So it's a good idea to make the relationship as good as it can be!

Bible: Psalm 133

David, who wrote this psalm, had seven brothers and many children.

Read Psalm 133

LEADER: But it's not easy in families. There are lots of tensions and often lots of arguments. As we're about to find out...

Drama: you've got to share

SHERRILL is sitting with her earphones on, singing, oblivious to the world. Next to her is a small table with a music centre or ghetto blaster on it. There is also a dirty mug, placed carefully on a CD, which is being used as a coaster.

Enter SHANE.

SHANE: Sherrill! *(No response)* Sherrill!

There is still no response, so he walks over to SHERRILL, and, unseen by her, turns up her music to full blast. SHERRILL leaps up in shock.

SHERRILL: What did you do that for!

SHANE: I thought your ears might need syringing. Have you got my CD?

SHERRILL: Which one?

SHANE: My heavy metal compilation – *Now That's What I Call Mindless Head Banging vol. 174.*

SHERRILL: *(Defensively)* I... I'm not sure.

SHANE: But I only lent it to you yesterday. It can't have disappeared. I mean, what's happened to it? Has it spontaneously combusted? Or been abducted by aliens with a particular fondness for thrash metal?

SHERRILL looks around. Eventually she locates the CD. It is the CD which is being used as a coaster for her coffee.

SHERRILL: Here it is.

She hands it to Shane.

SHANE: Look at it!

SHERRILL: What?

SHANE: You've ruined it.

SHERRILL: I didn't do it.

SHANE: Well, who did then?

SHERRILL: I dunno. It wasn't like that this morning.

SHANE: No, and it wasn't like that before you used it as a place mat. You'll have to buy me a new one.

SHERRILL: But it was an accident!

SHANE: Oh, so that cup of coffee just flew through the air and miraculously landed on the CD?

SHERRILL: You borrow my things.

SHANE: Like what?

SHERRILL: Like my avocado and sardine face mask. And you never asked me if you could have it.

SHANE: Well... it helps me meditate. At least I give it back. Everything I lend you comes back ruined.

SHERRILL: Well, it's not as if it was very good. I mean, a load of great hairy men screaming into a microphone. Be reasonable.

SHANE: *(Angry)* I am being reasonable.

SHERRILL: You're not – you're shouting.

SHANE: *(Shouting)* I AM NOT SHOUTING! I AM JUST BEING REASONABLE IN A LOUD VOICE!

SHERRILL: Alright. I'm sorry.

SHANE: *(Trying to calm down)* Yes, you're always saying that, you're very good at saying 'sorry.'

SHERRILL: *(Playing a trump card)* I thought your lot were supposed to for-give.

SHANE: *(Annoyed)* Don't drag that into it. You're always saying that...

SHERRILL: Well they are, aren't they? Aren't Christians supposed to forgive one another? Doth it not saith in the Bible, 'Go Ye and Forgiveth thy Sistereth' ?

SHANE: It's always the same! Whenever you've ruined something of mine, you always try to make me feel guilty about it, as if it were my fault.

SHERRILL: I'm only telling you what you're always telling me. That Christian-ity helps you get on with people. That God forgives us.

SHANE: Yeah well, God never had his *Now That's What I Call Mindless Head Banging* CD turned into a cup holder, did he! *(Trying to calm things down)* Alright, maybe I'm not a very good Christian, but at least I try. At least I make an effort. You just lie there, sneering at everyone and scratching yourself.

SHERRILL: I've said I'm sorry.

SHANE: You're always saying that, Sherrill. You never make any attempt to be nice to us, not to Mum, Dad or anyone. You've always got to be the rebel. And family life's not like that, Sherrill. It's give and take, compromise.

SHERRILL: It's easy for you – they think you're perfect.

SHANE: Only because I give in occasionally.

SHERRILL: But they never let me do what I want to do. Everyone hates me.

SHANE: Of course they don't. Not hate exactly. 'Detest' perhaps...

SHERRILL: Very funny...

SHANE: Look, all you have to do is try to be pleasant. Just once. Go on.

SHERRILL smiles at him.

SHERRILL: OK.

SHANE: And that'll be ten quid for the CD...

He exits in a hurry as SHERRILL throws something at him

PairTalk: brothers and sisters

About Shane and Sherrill
▷ What did you think of the way Shane behaved?
▷ Was Sherrill's response reasonable?
▷ Should Christians be expected to rise above this sort of thing?
▷ Is it fair to expect Shane to forgive?

About brothers or sisters
▷ Is your brother or sister like Shane or Sherrill? If not, what are they like?
▷ What's good about your brother/sister? Think of as many good things as you can.

LEADER: If you have brothers or sisters here, why not let them know something good about themselves? Get a sticker and write one good thing about them on it. Then go and find your brother or sister and stick the sticker on them.

You can always allow people to take stickers away with them if their siblings are not present.

Watch it!

Game: sibling quizzing

LEADER: The argument between Shane and Sherrill is nothing new. As well as some very good friendships, the Bible records some bitter arguments between siblings. So let's find out how much you know about brothers and sisters in the Bible.

At this point, tell them that part (a) of each question requires a name, or names, as an answer. These names are scattered around the church (they could be stuck to the walls with blu-tack or hidden in other places). They need to go and look for the answers. Part (b) of each question requires a bit more Bible knowledge!

The names around the church are:
- ▷ *Cain and Abel*
- ▷ *Shem, Ham and Japheth*
- ▷ *Jacob and Esau*
- ▷ *Reuben, Judah, Levi, Dan, Issachar, Naphtali, Asher, Gad, Benjamin, Zebulun, Simeon*
- ▷ *James and Jude*
- ▷ *Simon*
- ▷ *James and John*
- ▷ *Mary and Martha*

Give them a few minutes to walk around and look at the names and complete their quiz sheet. Then bring them back to take them through the answers. If you want to put them in teams at this point and allocate points accordingly you can do so. A leader's version of the quiz (with all the answers!) can be found below. A photocopiable version of this quiz can be found on p.27.

Sibling Quizzing

1. Adam had two famous sons who had very different attitudes to worshipping God.

(a) What were their names? *A: Cain and Abel.*

(b) Which one killed the other one? *A: Cain killed Abel (Gen. 4.25).*

2. When Noah built his ark to escape the flood, he took his wife, his sons and their wives, and two of each animal.

(a) Who were Noah's three sons? *A: Shem, Ham and Japheth (Gen. 9 and 10).*

(b) Which one fathered the Israelites? *A: Abraham and Jesus trace their lineage from Shem. The term 'anti-semitism,' meaning 'hostility toward Jews,' comes from the name 'Shemites' or 'semites.'*

3. Abraham had two sons, Isaac and Ishmael. Then Isaac had twin sons who went their separate ways.

(a) What were their names? *A: Jacob and Esau.*

(b) How were they different in appearance? *A: Esau was the elder and was red and hairy. Jacob was born after him and was 'a smooth man'!*

4. Jacob gave his son, Joseph, a coat of many colours. But this made Joseph's brothers jealous.

(a) How many brothers can you name? *A: Reuben, Judah, Levi, Dan, Issachar, Naphtali, Asher, Gad, Benjamin, Zebulun, Simeon. These became the names of the tribes of Israel.*

(b) Who was the eldest? *A: Reuben. The famous 'coat of many colours' was probably a richly embroidered coat, maybe with strands of gold and silver woven in. The gift implied not only that he was the favourite, but maybe that Jacob was intending him to be the leader of the clan. No wonder his brothers were furious with him!*

5. Jesus had brothers and sisters. Two of them later became leaders of the early church and authors of New Testament books.

(a) What were their names? *A: James and Jude. Mark 6.3 actually names four brothers: James, Joseph, Judas (Jude), and Simon. James wrote the book of James. The author of Jude calls himself 'a brother of Jesus.'*

(b) Which one was the leader of the Jerusalem church? *A: James was the leader of the Jerusalem church (e.g. see Acts 15)*

6. When Andrew learned that Jesus was the promised Messiah, he straightaway took his brother to see him.

(a) What was his brother's name? *A: Simon (Jn. 1.35–44). A fisherman, Andrew had been a disciple of John the Baptist until he met Jesus.*

(b) What did Jesus change it to? *A: Peter (Mt. 16.18).*

7. Two more of Jesus' disciples were brothers and business partners. Jesus called them 'The Sons of Thunder.'

(a) Who were they? *A: James and John (Mk. 3.17). These impulsive sons of Zebedee were, with Peter, the disciples closest to Jesus. James was the first of the apostles to be martyred by King Herod Agrippa I (Acts 12.2) about AD 43.*

(b) What was their business? *A: They were fishermen with their father, Zebedee.*

8. One of Jesus' best friends was Lazarus, whom he raised from the dead. Lazarus had two sisters.

(a) What were their names? *A: Mary and Martha.*

(b) Where did they live? *A: Bethany, two miles east of Jerusalem.*

LEADER: One of those stories in particular illustrates how favouritism between brothers and sisters can lead to resentment. It's a very famous story. In fact, I've often thought it would make an excellent musical. Let's hear it now.

Drama: Joseph and his brothers

Taken from Genesis 37.1–36 CEV

NARRATOR: Jacob lived in the land of Canaan, where his father Isaac had lived, and this is the story of his family.

When Jacob's son Joseph was seventeen years old, he took care of the sheep with his brothers, the sons of Bilhah and Zilpah. But he was always telling his father all sorts of bad things about his brothers.

Jacob loved Joseph more than he did any of his other sons, because Joseph was born after Jacob was very old. Jacob had given Joseph a fancy coat to show that he was his favourite son, and so Joseph's brothers hated him and would not be friendly to him. One day, Joseph told his brothers what he had dreamed, and they hated him even more.

JOSEPH: Let me tell you about my dream. We were out in the field, tying up bundles of wheat. Suddenly my bundle stood up, and your bundles gathered around and bowed down to it.

BROTHER 1: Do you really think you are going to be king and rule over us?

NARRATOR: Now they hated Joseph more than ever because of what he had said about his dream. Joseph later had another dream.

JOSEPH: Listen to what else I dreamed. The sun, the moon, and eleven stars bowed down to me.

NARRATOR: When he told his father about this dream, his father became angry.

JACOB: What's that supposed to mean? Are your mother and I and your brothers all going to come and bow down in front of you?

NARRATOR: Joseph's brothers were jealous of him, but his father kept wondering about the dream. One day when Joseph's brothers had taken the sheep to a pasture near Shechem, his father Jacob said to him:

JACOB: I want you to go to your brothers. They are with the sheep near Shechem.

JOSEPH: Yes, sir.

JACOB: Go and find out how your brothers and the sheep are doing. Then come back and let me know.

NARRATOR: So he sent him from Hebron Valley. Joseph was near Shechem and wandering through the fields, when a man asked:

MAN: What are you looking for?

JOSEPH: I'm looking for my brothers who are watching the sheep. Can you tell me where they are?

MAN: They're not here any more. I overheard them say they were going to Dothan.

NARRATOR: So Joseph left and found his brothers in Dothan. But before he got there, they saw him coming and made plans to kill him.

BROTHER 2: Look, here comes the hero of those dreams! Let's kill him and throw him into a pit and say that some wild animal ate him. Then we'll see what happens to those dreams.

NARRATOR: Reuben heard this and tried to protect Joseph from them.

REUBEN: Let's not kill him. Don't murder him or even harm him. Just throw him into a dry well out here in the desert.

NARRATOR: Reuben planned to rescue Joseph later and take him back to his father. When Joseph came to his brothers, they pulled off his fancy coat and threw him into a dry well. As Joseph's brothers sat down to eat, they looked up and saw a caravan of Ishmaelites coming from Gilead. Their camels were loaded with all kinds of spices that they were taking to Egypt. So Judah said...

JUDAH: What will we gain if we kill our brother and hide his body? Let's sell him to the Ishmaelites and not harm him. After all, he is our brother.

NARRATOR: And the others agreed.

When the Midianite merchants came by, Joseph's brothers took him out of the well, and for twenty pieces of silver they sold him to the Ishmaelites who took him to Egypt.

When Reuben returned to the well and did not find Joseph there, he tore his clothes in sorrow. Then he went back to his brothers.

REUBEN: The boy is gone! What am I going to do?

NARRATOR: Joseph's brothers killed a goat and dipped Joseph's fancy coat in its blood. After this, they took the coat to their father.

BROTHER 3: We found this! Look at it carefully and see if it belongs to your son.

NARRATOR: Jacob knew it was Joseph's coat.

JACOB: It's my son's coat! Joseph has been torn to pieces and eaten by some wild animal.

NARRATOR: Jacob mourned for Joseph a long time, and to show his sorrow he tore his clothes and wore sackcloth. All of Jacob's children came to comfort him, but he refused to be comforted.

JACOB: No! I will go to my grave, mourning for my son.

NARRATOR: So Jacob kept on grieving. Meanwhile, the Midianites had sold Joseph in Egypt to a man named Potiphar, who was the king's official in charge of the palace guard.

Gordon's siblings

LEADER: So we can see that arguments between brothers and sisters have been going on for many years. Sometimes when a brother or a sister gets something that we don't have, we resent that, just as Joseph's brothers resented his coat. And sometimes these feelings can continue for years and years.

GORDON: I'll say they do!

LEADER: Gordon! Is that you?

GORDON: Brothers and sisters! Don't talk to me about brothers and sisters!

LEADER: Have you got brothers and sisters then?

GORDON: I have. In fact I saw them last night at a family reunion. It was my Uncle and Aunt's 450th Wedding Anniversary.

LEADER: That must have been fun.

GORDON: Well, it would have been if it weren't for Gerald.

LEADER: Who's Gerald?

GORDON: My brother. He is so stuck up. Just because he's on the outside of Salisbury Cathedral, he looks down on us.

LEADER: Well, I should think if you're on the outside of Salisbury Cathedral you look down on most people.

GORDON: I told him, I may not be on the outside of a tourist attraction, but at least pigeons don't nest in my ears. And the way he treats Glynnis.

LEADER: Who's Glynnis?

GORDON: Our sister. Just because her church isn't used for worship any more. He goes on and on about it. It's not her fault it got turned into a five bedroomed home. I blame *Grand Designs*.

LEADER: So how do you deal with the conflict?

GORDON: I deal with it as you would expect a British gargoyle to deal with it. I am icily polite to Gerald. Or Pigeon-ears as I like to call him.

LEADER: That doesn't sound very polite.

GORDON: Well, it's his fault.

LEADER: How long has this argument been going on now?

GORDON: Not long. About three hundred years. He's so immature.

LEADER: Why don't you talk to him about it?

GORDON: He wouldn't listen. That's the trouble, no-one listens to anyone.

LEADER: But shouldn't you try to solve it? *(Pause)* Gordon?

GORDON: Oh sorry, I wasn't listening.

LEADER: Gordon!! Typical I might as well talk to the wall. In fact, now I come to think of it, I was talking to the wall!

Try it!

Comment: sibling rivalry

LEADER: There are lots of reasons why arguments break out among families: children need to share parents' time, attention, and love; families need to work out how to share space and possessions. There are often big differences between brothers and sisters: in age or abilities, interests or gifts. There may be arguments over friends, or toys, or even just the TV remote control!

So, how can we help each other? Maybe like Jacob, we can give each other presents – only good presents, presents that include everyone. That might mean the gift of some privacy or space away from each other. Or of listening to each other. Maybe we could give the present of seeing each others' point of view. Perhaps we should share a gift of doing something we really enjoy together.

I wonder if things would have been different if Jacob had given a different gift to his son? Could Joseph have behaved differently? Why don't we get that family back together and see if they could address the situation a bit better?

Daisy Daytime: Help! My son's been eaten by a goat!

Enter Daisy Daytime. She introduces the theme of the programme and brings on Jacob first. Jacob should obviously be upset about what happened to Joseph. He should explain why he treated him better than all the rest – and be challenged on that.

? Questions for Jacob

▷ How did you lose your son?
▷ Why did you give that coat to Joseph?
▷ Did you talk to your other children about the situation?
▷ Did your behaviour caused jealousy among your children?
▷ Do you have any regrets about the way you treated him?
▷ Did you send Joseph to spy on his brothers?

Daisy then brings out one or more of the brothers. Naturally they should be very defensive and guarded in their replies. The brothers should reveal their dislike of Joseph, their resentment at the favouritism shown by Jacob, but they should not admit the truth about what happened.

Questions for the brothers

▷ Did you try to talk to your father about the situation?
▷ Why did you feel you had to get rid of Joseph?
▷ How did your father's treatment of Joseph make you feel?
▷ Tell me more about the whole 'eaten by a goat' incident.

Then, triumphantly, Daisy should bring out Joseph (now a slave in Egypt). Maybe build things up a bit with Jacob ('Would it surprise you to know that goats are not, in fact, carnivorous?')

? Questions for Joseph

▷ What actually happened?
▷ How could you have behaved differently?
▷ Why did your brothers hate you?
▷ Were you surprised at their reaction?
▷ What have you learned from this experience?
▷ How do you feel about your family now?

Daisy should then turn to the congregation and ask their advice. How would they have handled things differently?

DAISY: Well, that's all we have time for.

On the bad side, we've seen how sibling rivalry can result in grief, pain and the ruining of a perfectly innocent goat's reputation.

On the good side we've seen that it improves the ratings.

You've been watching the Daisy Daytime show. Goodbye, and remember, drive carefully.

Live it!

TakeAway: a timeshare card.

Now it's time for people to work out what they are going to do within their family.

Give people a postcard or index card. Then ask them to write down what gift they are going to share with their family.

You can use suggestions and ideas thrown up during the hotseating exercise. Or you could put any of the following ideas up on an ideas sheet, or on the OHP or Powerpoint:

▷ *Private time on own or with one of family*

▷ *Own room, bed or chair, drawers*

▷ *Family council meetings*

▷ *'Friends' night – one friend each per member of family per week*

▷ *'Golden' time with sibling*

▷ *Mums and girls or Dads and sons weekends*

▷ *Plan a Family Funday*

▷ *Take turns choosing one activity at weekends to do together*

▷ *Plan treats for each other, make a card, give a little homemade gift, help make favourite food.*

Prayer: for families in need

LEADER: Let's pray for families of all sorts around the world.

God, our Father, we remember before you families that are in need. As we picture them in our minds, please surround them with your love.

We pray for families who argue, who find it hard to speak to one another in love

(pause)

We pray for families who struggle to survive or who go to bed hungry

(pause)

We pray for families who find it hard to spend any time together

(pause)

We pray for families who are forced to leave their homes

(pause)

We pray for families trying to cope with the loss of one of their relations

(pause)

For all these people, Lord, we ask you would give them the comfort of your love.

Amen

Closing prayer

God, our Father,

Help each of us here to show compassion, patience, understanding and love to those in our families.

Help us to show kindness to one another and all we meet,

to show humility as we remember your glory and greatness.

Help us to be patient with each family member,

to show love to one another, and through that to demonstrate your love to others.

Help us to look outwards,

to embrace others who don't have families of their own, but who need a place to feel valued and loved.

We remember that you were at work in the life of Joseph and his family and, after many years, they were reunited and reconciled.

Send your Spirit to each member of the family:

young and old,

big and small,

man and woman,

boy and girl.

Help us to live in unity and harmony together,

exercising grace and forgiveness day by day.

Amen

SIBLING QUIZZING!

How much do you know about brothers and sisters in the Bible? Here's a quiz to get your Bible brains buzzing!

1. Adam had two famous sons who had very different attitudes to worshipping God.

    (a) What were their names?

    (b) Which one killed the other one?

2. When Noah built his ark to escape the flood, he took his wife, his sons and their wives, and two of each animal.

    (a) Who were Noah's three sons?

    (b) Which one fathered the Israelites?

3. Abraham had two sons, Isaac and Ishmael. Then Isaac had twin sons who went their separate ways.

    (a) What were their names?

    (b) How were they different in appearance?

4. Jacob gave his son, Joseph, a coat of many colours. But this made Joseph's brothers jealous.

    (a) How many brothers can you name?

    (b) Who was the eldest?

5. Jesus had brothers and sisters. Two of them later became leaders of the early church and authors of New Testament books.

    (a) What were their names?

    (b) Which one was the leader of the Jerusalem church?

6. When Andrew learned that Jesus was the promised Messiah, he straightaway took his brother to see him.

    (a) What was his brother's name?

    (b) What did Jesus change it to?

7. Two more of Jesus' disciples were brothers and business partners. Jesus called them 'The Sons of Thunder.'

    (a) Who were they?

    (b) What was their business?

8. One of Jesus' best friends was Lazarus, whom he raised from the dead. Lazarus had two sisters.

    (a) What were their names?

    (b) Where did they live?

Getting ready

A week (or more) before

Bible: Psalm 133

☐ request reader for Psalm

Drama: you've got to share

☐ allocate parts and rehearse

PairTalk: brothers and sisters

☐ put questions on notice sheet or Powerpoint

Game: sibling quizzing

☐ print out quiz sheets
☐ prepare name cards
☐ decide on method of marking and how to display

Drama: Joseph and his brothers

☐ photocopy parts and allocate and rehearse if necessary

Drama: Gordon's siblings

☐ Copy script

Daisy Daytime: Help! My son's been eaten by a goat!

☐ allocate parts and give background material for hotseating

TakeAway: a timeshare card.

☐ print timeshare cards
☐ gather table mats, pencils

An hour (or more) before

☐ Arrange seating and set

Drama: you've got to share

☐ Put props and costumes in place

Game: sibling quizzing

☐ Make sure quiz sheets are ready to be given out
☐ Put names up around church
☐ Have pencils or pens ready

Drama: Joseph and his brothers

☐ Make sure photocopies are in place.

Drama: Gordon's siblings

☐ Set-up for Gordon (microphone, statue, etc. as required)

TakeAway: a timeshare card

☐ Put cards in place

Family

Did.
Didn't.
Did.
Didn't.
Smack!

2. DID. DIDN'T. DID. DIDN'T. SMACK!

Aim: How to avoid and resolve arguments

Bible: Colossians 3.13; Luke 22.24–30

1. Want it!

The purpose here is to
▷ see what causes arguments
▷ admit to getting angry

We do this by asking people to
▷ watch a drama
▷ talk about arguments they've had recently

The tools we use are
▷ Drama: welcome (take 1)
▷ PairTalk: what winds you up?

2. Watch it!

The purpose here is to
▷ identify what causes arguments and how people behave during arguments
▷ look at what the Bible says about arguments

We do this by asking people to
▷ watch a replay of the drama
▷ listen to the Bible

The tools we use are
▷ Comment and replay of drama: welcome (take 1)
▷ Bible: Colossians 3.13; Luke 22.24–30

3. Try it!

The purpose here is to
▷ think of ways of dealing with arguments
▷ use biblical principles

We do this by asking people to
▷ listen to Gordon
▷ problem-solve in pairs
▷ learn a reconciliation strategy

The tools we use are
▷ Drama: Gordon's greatness
▷ Problem-solving: how do you reduce arguments?
▷ Comment: the five-point peace process

4. Live it!

The purpose here is to
▷ memorise the 'peace process'
▷ pray for forgiveness

We do this by asking people to
▷ use actions
▷ pray
▷ watch drama

The tools we use are
▷ TakeAway: memorise the five-point peace process
▷ Prayer: confession
▷ Drama: welcome (take 2)
▷ Closing prayer

Running order

When	What	Who
	Want it!	
	Drama: welcome (take 1)	
	PairTalk: what winds you up?	
	Watch it!	
	Comment and replay drama: welcome (take 1)	
	Bible: Colossians 3.13; Luke 22.24–30	
	Try it!	
	Drama: Gordon's greatness	
	Problem-solving groups: how do you reduce arguments?	
	Comment: the five-point peace process	
	Live it!	
	TakeAway: memorise the five point process	
	Prayer: confession	
	Drama: welcome (take 2)	
	Closing prayer	

Want it!

Drama: welcome (take 1)

Enter ONE. You will need four people for this drama. For maximum shock-effect it's good if they can be people who usually lead services. And it's even better if they are people who are known to be calm, gentle and generally holy!

ONE: Welcome to our service today, which is on the subject of arguments and family rows. What causes the arguments in your house? What do you do when you get annoyed?

Today we ask, is it OK to get angry? And how do we resolve such situations? I don't know if you can see on Powerpoint ... *(looks round to find that there is no Powerpoint. Speaking pointedly in the direction of TWO)* I said, I don't know if you can see on Powerpoint...

TWO: Are you looking at me?

ONE: Well, you're supposed to be doing Powerpoint for this service.

TWO: How come I always have to do Powerpoint? Why don't we ever see you do it? How come I never get to lead the service?

ONE: Well, probably it has something to do with talent.

TWO: That's a rotten thing to say. I'm a better service leader than you, and you know it.

ONE: You aren't.

TWO: I am.

They bicker like mad. THREE enters.

THREE: What's going on?

ONE: She won't do Powerpoint.

THREE: Typical!

TWO: What do you mean typical?

THREE: It's the lawnmower all over again. *(Explaining to LEADER)* She borrowed our lawnmower and she's never given it back.

TWO: What's that got to do with me not doing Powerpoint?

THREE: It has everything to do with it. It's all a question of attitude.

TWO: You're so stupid, you are.

THREE: I rest my case.

TWO: Stupid and smug.

THREE: I am neither stupid nor smug.

TWO: Yes, you are. You're both of them put together. You're... you're... smugpid.

THREE: I am not. I am lovably eccentric. *(Pointing to ONE)* He's stupid.

ONE: I am not stupid!

THREE: Of course you are. You're so stupid, you don't even realise how stupid you are, that's how stupid you are.

ONE: Oh, right, so that's how it is, is it?

THREE: Yes, that's how it is.

Enter FOUR. He walks across to ONE, takes out a pair of scissors and carefully, deliberately, cuts ONE's tie off.

FOUR: And **that's** for last week.

They descend into argument. Enter LEADER.

LEADER: STOP! *(Then to congregation)* As you can see, it's easy to argue. We all do it, even if we're involved in something like running a church service!

PairTalk: what winds you up?

▷ What things have made you argue recently?

Watch it!

Comment and replay of drama

LEADER: I think what we've just seen illustrates three of the major causes of arguments. Let's have a look at an action replay.

These small snippets of the sketch should be re-enacted as close as possible to the style of the original. To enhance the effect, the LEADER could use a TV remote.

TWO: How come I always have to do the OHPs? Why don't we ever see you do them? How come I never get to lead the service?

ONE: Well, probably it has something to do with talent.

▷ How would you describe what's going on here?

LEADER: Pride can cause a lot of arguments. Next, look at this little exchange.

THREE: It's the lawnmower all over again. She borrowed our lawnmower and she's never given it back.

▷ What's going on here?

LEADER: Obviously, she's bearing a grudge about an event that occurred some time ago. Finally, let's have a look at another excerpt.

THREE: I am not stupid.

TWO: Yes, you are.

THREE: I am not. I am lovably eccentric. He's stupid.

> **?** ▷ What's happening in that exchange?

LEADER: Sometimes arguments are caused by simple rudeness. There's no other word for it.

In the Bible shows us that even those who should know better often ended up arguing.

Paul had to write to a church in a place called Colossae.

Read Colossians 3.13

LEADER: That must have been frustrating for him, to find that followers of Jesus were behaving in that way. But then again, even Jesus had to deal with the same kind of issues, going on right under his nose. The disciples were arguing about who was the greatest, twenty years before Paul wrote to the Colossians. And on the actual night before Jesus died!

Read Luke: 22.24–30

Try it!

Gordon's greatness

LEADER: So you can see, even the disciples argued. And even the early church argued. So I guess we might think that arguments are bound to break out at some stage, because we're all human and we all do things wrong. Maybe what we should work out is a different way of dealing with arguments.

GORDON: Oi! What about me?

LEADER: What about you?

GORDON: My public want to hear from me. I'm the best. That's what I told all the other gargoyles – people come to see me. I'm first amongst gargoyles.

LEADER: And what do the others think about that?

GORDON: Well, they're not talking to me at the moment. We've had a bit of an argument about it. You see, they wanted to talk to people, like I do. They wanted to do this bit, but this is my bit. I'm the star, not them. Anyway, none of them even wanted to join my fan club.

LEADER: You're starting a fan club?

GORDON: Of course. I'm a star. I speak to people every month.

LEADER: Well, the vicar speaks to people every week, but he hasn't got a fan club

GORDON: *(Pause)* You amaze me. Anyway, he hasn't got my star quality and my charisma. That's what I told the other gargoyles. I said, I've got charisma and you haven't and I'm not sharing it.

LEADER: Don't you think you're being a bit bigheaded?

GORDON: That's exactly what all the others said – and now they won't talk to me.

LEADER: How do you feel about that?

GORDON: Well, I'm a bit upset really. But we've argued now and I don't know what to do about it.

LEADER: Why don't you just tell them you're sorry?

GORDON: I shouldn't have to apologise for my genius.

LEADER: You're got to compromise a bit, Gordon. Move a little.

GORDON: I'm made of stone. It's not easy to move at all.

LEADER: Well, I don't know how to help you. Maybe the people here will have some ideas.

Problem-solving groups: how do you reduce arguments?

▷ How would you solve Gordon's problem?
▷ How would you solve the problems of the worship leaders in the sketch?

Groups select a representative and feedback.

Or you can pick one or two individuals and get feedback that way.

Comment: the five-point peace process

LEADER: Once we've unravelled the situation, we want people to be friends again. So how do we do that? When arguments occur, we should all engage our whole selves in the peace process. And that means: ears, nose, heart, right hand, both hands. I call this the five-point peace process. *(Mark off on fingers of one hand)*

As the LEADER goes through the five-point peace process, get members of the congregation to touch their ears, nose, heart and hands as appropriate.

If possible have another voice to read out the Bible verses.

First, the ears. *(point to your ear)*

Slow down for a minute – listen to the other point of view.

This is what James says in the Bible:

READER: My dear friends, you should be quick to listen and slow to speak or to get angry. If you are angry, you cannot do any of the good things that God wants done (Jas. 1.19–20).

LEADER: **Next, the nose.** *(take a deep breath)*

Take a deep breath – let kindness replace anger. This is what Proverbs says:

READER: A kind answer soothes angry feelings, but harsh words stir them up (Prov. 15.1).

LEADER: **Then the heart.** *(hand on heart)*

Say sorry or forgive people – whichever is appropriate. God is our Father, and He wants us to love each other. Saying sorry shows that we understand this. John says:

READER: Love each other. Just as I have loved you (Jn. 13.34).

LEADER: And Paul wrote to the church in Colossae:

READER: Bear with each other and forgive whatever grievances you may have against one another. Forgive as the Lord forgave you. (Col. 3.13).

LEADER: **Then our right hand.** *(shake on it)*

We should make up – be friends again. Jesus said:

READER: Blessed are the peacemakers for they will be called sons of God (Mt. 5.6).

LEADER: **Finally both hands.** *(make a pillow with hands)*

We should put it behind us – and go to bed happy.

Paul writes:

READER: Don't get so angry that you sin. Don't go to bed angry and don't give the devil a chance (Eph. 4.26–7).

Live it!

TakeAway: memorise the five-point peace process

LEADER: So, arguments will happen. They happen in the best of families, and even in church. They even happened among Jesus' disciples! But the Bible shows us things we can do. Let's remember the five-point peace process.

1. Ears: see the other point of view *(point to your ear)*
2. Nose: make room for kindness *(take a deep breath)*
3. Heart: say sorry *(hand on heart)*
4. Right hand: make up *(shake on it)*
5. Both hands: go to bed happy *(make a pillow with hands)*

And if you have trouble with any part of the process, take the problem back to God and ask him to help you deal with it.

Remember, God is very forgiving towards us. The Bible tells us that over and again.

Psalm 103.8 says: 'The Lord is merciful! He is kind and patient, and his love never fails.'

We all do bad things sometimes. The good thing is, we can tell God what we've done and how we're feeling. God will always listen when we say sorry. He makes us feel better.

Prayer: confession

Lord God,

We come before you now to say sorry.

Instead of walking humbly, we strut around proudly.

Instead of forgiving people, we carry our grudges for a long time.

Instead of speaking peaceably, we are rude and angry.

Forgive us, Lord, for the things we do that lead to arguments and fights; in our families, in our church and elsewhere in our lives.

Help us, instead, to look to your son, Jesus,

Who walked humbly on earth as a man,

Who forgave people – even those who put him to death,

Who spoke words of peace and asked us to love our enemies.

Amen

Drama: welcome (take 2)

ONE: Welcome to our service today, which is on the subject of arguments. I don't know if you can see on Powerpoint (*looks round to find that there is no Powerpoint*). I said, I don't know if you can see on Powerpoint.

TWO: Look, can I just say something? I'm happy to do Powerpoint, but do you think I could have a go at leading the service in the future?

ONE: Of course, if you'd like to. I suppose it should really have been your turn this time.

TWO: No, no, that's all right. It's not a matter of turns. Now, where's the laptop?

Enter THREE

THREE: (*Whispers*) Er – before you start, I just wondered if you'd finished with the lawnmower yet.

TWO: Oh, I'm sorry – of course I have.

THREE: Only I think I've persuaded my husband to do the grass for the first time in eleven years of marriage, so it would be a shame to miss the opportunity.

ONE: Don't you think we ought to be getting on?

THREE: OK. Sorry – typical me, slowing things down.

Enter FOUR with a pair of scissors. He goes up to ONE, grabs his tie and then just snips a tiny piece of cotton from the bottom.

ONE: (*Surprised*) Thanks.

FOUR: Don't mention it.

ONE: So, let's start the service...

LEADER: STOP!! You're too late. It's time for coffee and biscuits. But isn't it a lot better when we don't argue?

Closing prayer

Lord Jesus,
Lead us forward from here
to walk the path of peace;
to help each other along the way
with patience, kindness and understanding.
Help us to put aside what we want
and to follow in your footsteps instead.
Amen

Getting ready

A week (or more) before

Drama: welcome (take 1 and 2)

☐ allocate parts and rehearse

PairTalk: brothers and sisters

☐ put question on notice sheet or Powerpoint

Drama: Gordon's greatness

☐ Copy script

An hour (or more) before

☐ Arrange seating and set

Drama: welcome (take 1 and 2)

☐ Put props and costumes in place

Drama: Gordon's greatness

☐ Set-up for Gordon (microphone, statue, etc. as required)

Mum's the word!

3. MUM'S THE WORD!

Aim: To thank God for the love of mothers, and to refresh and encourage them

Bible: 1 Corinthians 13.4–7; 1 John 4.16b

1. Want it!

The purpose here is to
▷ get people to listen to statements about God's love
▷ describe their own mothers

We do this by asking people to
▷ stand and listen
▷ sit and talk

The tools we use are:
▷ Stand up and listen: the mother love of God
▷ PairTalk: describe your mother

2. Watch it!

The purpose here is to
▷ find out the highs and lows of being a mum
▷ hear what love is like

We do this by asking people to
▷ listen to a mother's job description
▷ hear real mums' experiences
▷ listen to the Bible

The tools we use are
▷ Comment: job description for a mum
▷ Interview: highs and lows of being a mum
▷ Bible: 1 Corinthians 13.4–7

3. Try it!

The purpose here is to
▷ see how much love mums need
▷ get people to think about how loving they are

We do this by asking people to
▷ watch a scene from family life
▷ discuss Sheila's attitude
▷ relook at 1 Corinthians 13.4–7

The tools we use are
▷ Drama: Sherrill needs dosh
▷ Discussion: Sheila's attitude
▷ Bible: fill the blanks
▷ Prayers: silent confession and 'I want to be like you'

4. Live it!

The purpose here is to
▷ thank mums
▷ reflect on God's love

We do this by asking people to
▷ listen to Gordon
▷ give and receive flowers
▷ listen to a meditation

The tools we use are
▷ Comment: share the love
▷ Beat it: love the Lord your God
▷ Drama: Gordon's mum
▷ TakeAway: flowers for mums
▷ Meditation: spring flowers
▷ Closing prayer

Running order

When	What	Who
	Want it!	
	Stand up and listen: the mother love of God	
	PairTalk: describe your mother	
	Watch it!	
	Comment: job description for mum	
	Interviews: highs and lows of being a mum	
	Bible: 1 Corinthians 13.4–7	
	Try it!	
	Drama: Sherrill needs dosh	
	Discussion: Sheila's attitude	
	Bible: fill the blanks	
	Prayers: silent confession and 'I want to be like you'	
	Live it!	
	Comment: share the love	
	Beat it: love the Lord your God	
	Drama: Gordon's mum	
	TakeAway: flowers	
	Meditation: spring flowers	
	Closing prayer	

Want it!

LEADER: Welcome to today's service, in which we think about our mothers, their love for us, and the mother love of God.

Stand up and listen: the mother love of God

The whole of the Bible is one long song
to the unfailing love of God.
Stand up everyone and listen!
Listen to what our God is like:
His love reaches higher than the heavens;
his loyalty extends beyond the clouds.[1]
Nothing in all creation can separate us from
God's love for us in Christ Jesus our Lord.[2]
Neither trouble nor suffering, hard times nor hunger,
nakedness, danger or death.[3]
He will comfort you, like a mother comforting her child,
The prophet Isaiah tells us:
He will not turn away and forget us,[4]
For he himself has said to Jerusalem,
Could a mother forget a child who nurses at her breast?
Could she fail to love an infant who comes from her own body?
Even if a mother could forget, the Lord says, I will never forget you.
A picture of your city is drawn on my hand.
You are always in my thoughts.[5]
We join the song of prophets and kings,
of parents and children who can say: God is love.
Lord, like a young child on its mother's lap,
With you, we feel safe and satisfied.[6]

---

[1] *Psalm 57.10;* [2] *Romans 8.39;* [3] *Romans 8.35;* [4] *Isaiah 66.13;* [5] *Isaiah 49.15-16;* [6] *Psalm 131.2*

PairTalk: Describe your mother

?
▷ What is your mother like?
▷ Or what memories do you have of your mother?

Watch it!

Job description: mother

LEADER: We've talked about what our own mothers are like, and of course, they're all very different. But they've all got the same job. So what does a mother do? What would her job description be?

The following can be read by the LEADER, or by another voice.

READER: Position vacant: Mother needed.

This is a challenging position offering long-term, indeed permanent work.

Candidates must be willing to work long and variable hours, and are on call at all times of the day and night, especially during the induction process of new members to the family. Includes some weekend work. Well, quite a lot of weekend work, actually.

Some overnight travel is required, which includes visits to campsites, casualty departments and bleak, windswept beaches. Candidates will also be required to attend school plays, concerts, sports days and other occasions. Some video-taping skills may be a bonus.

Successful applicants will be responsible for a variety of training tasks, including nose-blowing, lace-tying, hair-combing and toilet training. Some of these tasks will need to be repeated throughout the trainee's career.

The successful candidate will demonstrate the negotiating skills of a diplomat, the crisis management skills of a Brigadier General and the conflict resolution skills of a UN peacekeeper.

An ability to create craft projects out of only a used cornflake box and a bit of sellotape would be an advantage, as would the ability to co-ordinate diaries, project manage homework, run a taxi-service and organise a wide-range of social gatherings.

Candidates will be expected to keep their temper, and withstand the desire to say 'I told you so', even though, apparently, they are always wrong.

Above all, the candidates will be need to be always ready, always caring, always patient, always listening and always indispensable.

Salary: negotiable. *(Correcting mistake)* Sorry, negligible.

Interview: highs and lows of being a mum

Choose a mother from your congregation and ask her to share her experiences.

▷ Did any of that description chime with you?
▷ What's the best bit about being a mum?
▷ What's been the hardest bit so far?
▷ What has God taught you through being a mum?

Bible: 1 Corinthians 13.4–7

LEADER: I wonder if many of us would answer a job advert like that. Mums need a lot of stamina and energy, but in order to keep going they need a lot of love. What is love? Let's hear what Paul had to say.

Read 1 Corinthians 13.4–7

LEADER: That's an amazing description of love, and we'll think about that a bit more in a minute.

But we all know that life isn't often as loving as that, and that sometimes the relationship between a mum and her children can get pretty difficult. Let's visit the Shaw family now, and see what the mum, Sheila, and her daughter, Sherrill, are up to.

Try it!

Drama: Sherrill needs some dosh

SHEILA is sitting reading Hello *magazine.*

Enter SHERRILL. She is wearing outrageous make-up and wears an outfit of mainly torn clothing.

SHERRILL: Mum...

SHEILA: *(Not looking up)* Yes?

SHERRILL: Can you lend me some money?

SHEILA: *(In a voice that indicates she has been asked this a million times)* What for?

SHERRILL: I promised Jan I'd go to the pictures with her tonight.

SHEILA: What happened to your pocket money?

SHERRILL: I spent it. I only want a loan till next week.

SHEILA: Well, I'm not sure... *(looking up)* Oh my goodness! What happened?

SHERRILL: What?

SHEILA: Your lips. What happened to your lips?

SHERRILL: It's lipstick.

SHEILA: It's horrible. Look at you! You can't want to look like that.

SHERRILL: Course I do. I think it looks good.

SHEILA: How can anyone in their right mind think that that looks good?

SHERRILL: Wayne thinks it looks good.

SHEILA: I said 'in their right mind'. I'm not sure your boyfriend falls into that category.

SHERRILL: You don't understand.

SHEILA: I understand all right. I understand that you never listen to a word I say. All I ask is that you pay a little attention to me, give me a little respect. I am your mother after all. I do have some experience of the world.

SHERRILL: Why should I listen to you? You never listen to me.

SHEILA: That's because you talk rubbish. I don't understand this, really I don't. You never used to be like this.

SHERRILL: When?

SHEILA: When you were six. Oh, you were so lovely. You used to sit on my lap and I'd read you stories. We'd watch videos together and you'd dress like your favourite characters – Cinderella and Sleeping Beauty. *(Looking at SHERRILL, and more tearful)* Now, apparently, your favourite film is the *Texas Chainsaw Massacre...*

SHERRILL: *(Annoyed)* I don't know why you moan about what I wear. I don't mind what you wear.

SHEILA: That's because I don't go out looking like... like *(whispers)* a tart.

SHERRILL: What flavour?

SHEILA: Don't you be so cheeky.

SHERRILL: Well, that's not a very nice thing to say, is it? You wouldn't like it if I said things like that about you.

SHEILA: Well, if you think I'm going to give you money to go out dressed like that, you're very much mistaken.

SHERRILL: Oh, Mum!

SHEILA relents a little, suddenly spotting an opportunity for a little bargaining.

SHEILA: I'll give it to you, if... if you comb your hair.

SHERRILL: Comb my hair? It took me hours to get it like this.

SHEILA: You look like you've had a nasty shock. You look like your grand-mother did the day her hearing aid exploded. You can have the money if you comb your hair and wear a pair of jeans.

SHERRILL: I am wearing jeans.

SHEILA: You are not. You are wearing a series of holes loosely tied together with denim.

SHERRILL: Oh forget it – it's not worth the hassle. I'll borrow the money from someone else!

Exit SHERRILL

Discussion: what would you say?

▷ If you were the mum here, what would you do or say?
▷ Do you think Sheila and Sherrill are being loving towards one another?

Bible: fill in the blanks

LEADER: Let's go back to Paul's list about love. And this time, you'll see there are some missing words.

Hand out pieces of paper or card with the following on it. Or you could put it in your church notice sheet.

.... is kind and patient, never jealous, boastful, proud, or rude.

.... isn't selfish or quick-tempered.

.... doesn't keep a record of wrongs that others do.

.... rejoices in the truth, but not in evil.

.... is always supportive, loyal, hopeful, and trusting.

.... never fails!

Get people to write their name on the dotted line.

LEADER: Are you like that? It's a big ask, isn't it? In fact, I think that's a pretty good description of the ideal mum. But Paul wasn't writing just for mums: we're *all* supposed to be like that. Look at this description of love now, and let's have a moment's silence to talk to God about whether we can honestly say these things about ourselves.

Prayer: silent confession

Give people time to think about how they love people, what they do well, what they have difficulty doing, and to ask God's forgiveness and help to carry on.

Prayer: I want to be like you

LEADER: Lord, you are patient and kind and hopeful.

ALL: I want to be like you.

LEADER: Never jealous or rude or proud or boastful.

ALL: I want to be like you.

LEADER: You aren't quick-tempered or selfish or vengeful.

ALL: I want to be like you.

LEADER: You don't rejoice in evil but love truth to win.

ALL: I want to be like you.

LEADER: You're supportive, and loyal, and trusting, too.

ALL: I want to be like you.

LEADER: You never fail and nor does your love.

ALL: I want to be like you.

LEADER: We want to be like you, Lord.

ALL: Help us to love like you.

Live it!

Comment: share the love

LEADER: God wants everyone to love him and others wholeheartedly. The commandments originally given to the people of Israel were all about doing this. Jesus summed them up in this way:

'Love the Lord your God with all your heart and with all your soul and with all your strength. Love your neighbour as yourself' (Luke 10.27).

God wants us to share these principles with our families.

'These commandments that I give you today are to be upon your hearts. Impress them on your children. Talk about them when you sit at home, and when you walk along the road, when you lie down and when you get up' (Deut 6.6–7).

So let's remember to do that: Mums – and Dads – and everyone else.

Beat it: 'love the Lord your God' refrain

Count to four to establish the rhythm and pace, then lead by saying part A. The stress in the first and second lines should fall on the words 'Love', 'God', 'heart' and 'strength'. The congregation responds with part B. Once they've got the hang of it, you can split the congregation into two parts (A & B).

A: Love the Lord your God, with all your heart and soul and strength.
B: Love the Lord your God, with all your heart and soul and strength.
A: When you're sitting down at home – [CLAP!]
B: Love the Lord your God!
A: When you're walking down the road – [CLAP!]
B: Love the Lord your God!
A: When you're lying on your bed – [CLAP!]
B: Remember what was said – [CLAP!]
All: Love the Lord your God with all your heart and soul and strength!

B: Love your neighbour too, never jealous, proud or rude.
A: Love your neighbour too, never jealous, proud or rude.
B: When you're sitting down at home – [CLAP!]
A: Love your neighbour too!
B: When you're walking down the road – [CLAP!]
A: Love your neighbour too!
B: When you're lying on your bed – [CLAP!]
A: Remember what was said – [CLAP!]
All: Love your neighbour too, never jealous, proud or rude!

LEADER: Great! Now one more time, here's a reminder for the mums today:

B: Talk about the Lord, with your children, noon and night.

A: Talk about the Lord, with your children, noon and night.

B: When you're sitting down at home – [CLAP!]

A: Talk about the Lord!

B: When you're walking down the road – [CLAP!]

A: Talk about the Lord!

B: When you're lying on your bed – [CLAP!]

B: Remember what was said – [CLAP!]

A: Talk about the Lord, with your children, noon and night!

Gordon's mum

LEADER: I wonder how many of you have given flowers to your mothers today?

GORDON: I have.

LEADER: Gordon? Is that you?

GORDON: Yes. I've given flowers to my Mum. Well, not flowers, actually. Gargoyles don't really do flowers. But I gave her a lovely bunch of moss and lichen. I was watching that sketch and it reminded me of my youth. We used to argue all the time when I was a teenager.

LEADER: You were a teenager?

GORDON: Of course. Although for gargoyles the teenage years tend to be between 100 and 180. I remember her reaction when I dyed my beard blue. She got her own back, though.

LEADER: What did she do?

GORDON: She dyed her beard purple. I used to stay up all night, listening to music.

LEADER: What music do young gargoyles like, then?

GORDON: Heavy rock, of course. I used to play my music really loud, and then Mum would come across to my ledge and tell me to turn it down. And you know I'd look at her and think of all she'd done for me... and then turn it up.

LEADER: That's not very nice.

GORDON: Well, I was young! I was only 165. I was rebellious. Anyway, she gave as good as she got. She used to wait till I was asleep early in the morning and start singing her favourite hymns at full volume.

LEADER: Sounds like you didn't get on very well.

GORDON: Not then. But all families go through that. She's lovely, my mum.

LEADER: I'm sure she is. Does she live near here?

GORDON: No, she's in the gargoyle's retirement home. Or Westminster Abbey as it's otherwise known. She's happy up there, making faces at the tourists and listening to the clergy argue with one another. She says it's just like the old days in the Reformation. Only without the bonfires.

LEADER: Right. Well, anyway, do give her my regards when you go and see her. You can take her some more flowers. They'll go nicely with her beard.

TakeAway: flowers

It may be the tradition in your church to give out posies of flowers to the mums. (Even if it isn't your tradition, perhaps now's the time to start it!)

Ask one child from each family to come and collect a posy and take it to their mum. Ask remaining siblings to offer flowers to the other women in the congregation who may be mums or grans. All of them, of course, are daughters of other mums!

Meditation: spring flowers

LEADER: If you've been given some flowers, hold them up high.
Lord, these spring flowers – the colour of sunshine – are glorious.
So bright, so cheerful, they light up the room!
On our streets, in our gardens, in unexpected places,
these outposts of sunshine silently declare your glory.

Now look at them closely. Feel the petals.
They are soft and smooth,
yet when buffeted by wind and rain,
they are sturdy and strong.
Your word is even stronger, Lord,
and your love endures forever.

Hold up your flowers again and wave them in the air!
Like flowers growing on the banks by a stream,
We ask you, Lord, to water us with your life-giving words and love.
May the colour and joy of your Spirit in us
refresh the world around us and shine in our homes.

Closing prayer

God, you heap your love upon us
like a mother providing for her family's needs,
embracing her children with tenderness.
Forgive us when, like spoilt children,
we treat your generosity as our right,
or hug it possessively to ourselves.
Give us enough trust to live secure in your love
and to share it freely with others,
in open-handed confidence
that your grace will never run out.
Amen

Might come in handy

About Mother's Day

Mother's Day is celebrated throughout the world – although on different days of the year. The Romans had a day – *Matronalia* – that was dedicated to Juno, when mothers were usually given gifts.

Recent practice in the USA grew out of the Civil War and was linked to a call for peace. Social activist Julia Ward Howe called for a day to unite women against war. Nowadays it has lost this 'peace' tag and is purely a celebration of motherhood.

In the UK 'Mothering Sunday' grew from a different source. Some people trace it back as far as the sixteenth century, where workers who had moved from their home would visit their 'mother' church once a year. This meant that mothers would be reunited with their children, many of whom had moved away to become apprentices or servants.

Getting ready

A week (or more) before

PairTalk: describe your mother

- [ ] Put questions on Powerpoint/ notice sheet
- [ ] Prepare interviewee with discussion questions

Interview: highs and lows of being a mum

- [ ] Ask interviewee and discuss aims

Drama: Sherrill needs some dosh

- [ ] Allocate parts and rehearse

Prayers: 'I want to be like you'

- [ ] Put prayers on notice sheet/ Powerpoint

Beat it: love the Lord your God

- [ ] Photocopy parts and rehearse

Drama: Gordon's mum

- [ ] Photocopy script

TakeAway: flowers for mums

- [ ] Order flowers

An hour (or more) before

- [ ] Arrange seating and set

Drama: Sherrill needs some dosh

- [ ] Put props and costumes in place

Drama: Gordon's mum

- [ ] Set-up for Gordon (microphone, statue, etc. as required)

TakeAway: flowers

- [ ] Put flowers in place

Family

Tidy up your room!

4. TIDY UP YOUR ROOM!

Aim: To encourage people to serve one another at home

Bible: Galatians 5.22–6.10

1. Want it!

The purpose here is to
▷ hear about God the servant
▷ think about how families share the workload at home

We do this by asking people to
▷ listen
▷ discuss in pairs

The tools we use are
▷ Stand up and listen: the servant God
▷ PairTalk: who does the chores?

2. Watch it!

The purpose here is to
▷ find out what the Bible says about our attitudes to each other

We do this by asking people to
▷ watch a drama
▷ think about how we should act as Christians

The tools we use are
▷ Drama: tidy up your room!
▷ Bible: Galatians 5.22–6.10

3. Try it!

The purpose here is to
▷ think through how to apply Paul's teaching at home
▷ share good ways to work together

We do this by asking people to
▷ question the characters
▷ give the Shaw family advice

The tools we use are
▷ Daisy Daytime: Help! My son's a couch potato!

4. Live it!

The purpose here is to
▷ help people do as Paul says at home

We do this by asking people to
▷ pray
▷ find new ways of serving

The tools we use are
▷ Drama: Gordon's mossy ears
▷ TakeAway: chore chart
▷ Prayer: thanks for those who serve us
▷ Closing prayer

Running order

When	What	Who
	Want it!	
	Stand up and listen: God the servant	
	PairTalk: who does the chores?	
	Watch it!	
	Drama: tidy up your room!	
	Bible: Galatians 5.22–6.10	
	Try it!	
	Daisy Daytime: Help! My son's a couch potato!	
	Live it!	
	Drama: Gordon's mossy ears	
	TakeAway: chore chart	
	Prayers: thanks for those who serve us	
	Closing prayer	

Want it!

LEADER: Welcome to our service today. Today we get right down to earth and discuss chores. Who does them? Who likes doing them? And which ones do we always leave until last? We'll be seeing if the Bible has anything to say on the subject.

Stand up and listen: the servant God

Stand up everybody and listen.
Listen to what our God is like:
He is a king, a leader, a lord,
but he is also a waiter, a cleaner, a cook.
Read the gospels and see if it's not true:
Christ was truly God,
but he did not try to remain equal with God.
Instead he gave up everything
and became a slave,
when he became like one of us.[1]
He is our king, our leader, our lord,
but he is also our waiter, our cleaner, our cook.
He calls us to be servants, not masters.
He calls us to be like him:
Leaders like to order their people around
And have power over everyone they rule.
But Jesus didn't act like them.
He did not come to be a slave master,
but to give his life as a slave
to rescue many people.[2]
He is our king, our leader, our lord,
but he is also our waiter, our cleaner, our cook.

[1] Philippians 2.7–8; [2] Matthew 20.25b–28

PairTalk: who does the chores?

?
▷ Which household jobs do you quite enjoy doing?
▷ Which household chores would you rather leave to someone else?
▷ If a Martian were to observe your family life, what do you think he'd have to say about it?
▷ What would you most like to change?

Watch it!

Drama: tidy up your room!

*Once again we are with the SHAW family. SHANE – the teenage boy
– is slouched in a chair, watching TV. Enter his father, SEAN.*

SEAN: The lawn needs cutting. *(There is no response from SHANE)* I said, the lawn needs cutting.

SHANE: I heard you.

SEAN: Well?

SHANE: Well, what?

SEAN: You don't care, do you? You never even lift a finger, except to pick your nose.

SHANE: Well, it's not my fault the lawn needs cutting. It's not my lawn.

SEAN: Oh, and that makes it all right, I suppose?

SHANE: Oh, don't go on at me, Dad. I've had a hard day.

SEAN: Listen, when I was your age I used to have to do all kinds of things around the house. I used to have to clean out the oven on my knees before I went to school.

SHANE: What did you have an oven on your knees for?

SEAN: Then I used to clean out the chicken house.

SHANE: Well, that's it then. I'll go and clean out the chicken house. Oh, I forgot, we haven't got one.

SEAN: Don't you be so cheeky young man or you'll be laughing on the other side of your face. *(Totally changing approach and trying to sweet talk him)* Look, mate, we don't ask for much, do we? Just do the occasional chore, maybe tidy up your room.

SHANE: I did my room yesterday.

SEAN: *(Giving up immediately on the sweet-talking style)* Well, you can't have cleaned it properly. Your mother says it looks like a pigsty.

SHANE: Mother's neurotic.

SEAN: Don't you speak about your mother like that. Anyway, that's not the point. It still needs cleaning.

SHANE: I'll do it after this programme.

SEAN: What programme?

SHANE: I'm watching TV.

SEAN: But that's *Thomas the Tank Engine*.

SHANE: So? I like *Thomas the Tank Engine*.

SEAN: Shane, you're fifteen. You should have outgrown this by now.

SHANE: Look, I've said I'll do it.

SEAN: We're not asking you for much, you know. Just clean up your room and do your washing.

SHANE: I did my washing last Tuesday.

SEAN: Which last Tuesday was that? The last Tuesday in 1991, perhaps? The last Tuesday in the tenth century?

SHANE: I'm a very clean boy.

SEAN: There is no such thing. It's started to live, that linen bin of yours. David Attenborough will be here any day soon to film it walking around.

SHANE: I'll do it.

SEAN: *Now.*

SHANE: *(Desperately trying to find an excuse, and overacting badly)* I'm not feeling well...

SEAN: Oh, what a shame. All of a sudden he's not feeling well.

SEAN strokes SHANE's forehead tenderly, then slaps his forehead.

SHANE: Ouch!

SEAN: Now.

SHANE: *(Trying to escape)* I need to go to the loo...

SEAN grabs SHANE as he rushes past and pulls him back.

SEAN: Oh no, I'm not having you climb out of the toilet window again.

SHANE: But I'm desperate!

SEAN: *(Shouting)* No, *I'm* desperate! You are going to do the lawn. You are not going to the toilet or suddenly succumbing to beri-beri, or watching the adventures of a load of talking steam trains. You will mow the lawn!

SHANE: *(Pause. He is defeated)* Oh, all right then.

Reluctantly he starts to leave the room. Then, his attention is caught by something on the TV.

SHANE: Hang on a minute.

SEAN: What is it now?

SHANE: Look – the *Tweenies!*

SHANE returns to the TV. FATHER exits.

Bible: Galatians 5.22–6.10

LEADER: I won't ask if you have arguments like that in your house! But there are always more than enough jobs that need doing – so who's going to do them?

How should we act as Christians? Let's see what Paul had to say. He wrote a letter to the churches in Galatia – an area that today we would call mid-Turkey. It was one of the first places where he preached the gospel to Gentiles. He founded three churches, in Derbe, Lystra and Iconium, and he wrote this letter to help them understand what it meant to follow Jesus.

Reads from Galatians 5.22–6.10

> **?** ▷ What are some of the things that Paul says?

LEADER: Now Paul isn't writing about chores, exactly, but about the love and grace of Jesus, and that's how we should operate in our daily lives.

Paul is telling us to help others and to share the workload. That's true whether we're talking about jobs in the home or jobs in church.

I think it's time to talk to the people we saw arguing earlier. And that means it's time for the Daisy Daytime Show.

Try it!

Daisy Daytime: Help! My son is a couch potato!

For more information on Daisy Daytime see p.11.

Enter Daisy Daytime. She introduces the title of the show and brings out Sean first.

Sean could give us more details about the hardship of his youth:

▷ *When I was young, I had to pick potatoes at 5am every morning. It never did me any harm.*

▷ *Anyway he's got to do as I say. I'm his father.*

▷ *Even quote Ephesians 5.6....*

? Questions for Sean
▷ Question: Sean, why do you expect Shane to mow the lawn?
▷ Do you always ask him to do jobs in that way?
▷ Shouldn't he be allowed to do what he wants in his own room?
▷ What are you going to do now if he doesn't do what you ask?
▷ How did you feel about the chores when you were younger?
▷ What do you do around the house?

Daisy then introduces Shane. Shane could reveal more about his father's behaviour and more elaborate excuses about why he can't do his chores.

▷ *Jesus told Mary she was right to sit down and put her feet up.*

▷ *If I do chores, I get sweaty and that leads to global warming.*

▷ *I'm not well.*

▷ *I need to save strength for more important things, like football.*

▷ *And anyway, the rest of the verse Dad quotes says, 'Parents don't exasperate your children', etc...*

> **?** **Questions for Shane**
> ▷ Shane, why don't you get up and mow the lawn right now?
> ▷ Why don't you tidy up your room? Isn't it only fair that you should?
> ▷ Why do you keep putting off these chores?
> ▷ Are you going to cut the lawn?
> ▷ What do you do around the house?

Finally Daisy Daytime asks the congregation to solve this. What do they think Sean and Shane should do?

> **?** **Questions for both of them**
> ▷ What did you think of the Bible passage read just now?
> ▷ Do you put it into practice?
> ▷ How do you share out the jobs in your house?
> ▷ How do you think they ought to be shared out?
> ▷ Do you exasperate one another?
> ▷ How often do you argue about chores?
> ▷ Which members of your family like being tidy?

DAISY: Well, that's all we have time for. On the bad side, we've seen how arguments over chores can bring chaos, destruction and ruin to the lives of a family. Or at least make life a bit of a pain. But on the good side, we've seen that it makes great TV. You've been watching the Daisy Daytime show. Goodbye, and, remember, always wear a vest.

Daisy and the other characters exit.

Live it!

Drama: Gordon's mossy ears

LEADER: So we've seen how difficult it can be to get things done around the house. And we've heard Paul's advice to the Galatians on how they should act as followers of Jesus. We've offered advice to Sean and Shane Shaw. Now, perhaps it's time to think about our own situation. Are there things you know you're supposed to do in your house? Are there ways in which you can help?

GORDON: Excuse me!

LEADER: Hello, Gordon, I was wondering when you'd turn up.

GORDON: It's not just at home you know. There are lots of chores and jobs to be done around here.

LEADER: Are there?

GORDON: Take my ears.

LEADER: Pardon?

GORDON: My ears. They need unblocking.

LEADER: Do they?

GORDON: Yes. I've got moss growing in them. But does anyone care? Oh no. And my back hasn't been dusted for ages.

LEADER: Well, can't you do this kind of thing yourself?

GORDON: No, it's very difficult to reach when you're a gargoyle. And anyway, I'm a star! You can't expect me to do chores. I'm supposed to hang around and look decorative. That's my job.

LEADER: Yes, well, let's just hope you're not on performance-related pay.

GORDON: I'll pretend I didn't hear that. In fact, I don't even have to pretend because there's so much moss in my ears.

LEADER: Well, can't you get one of the other gargoyles to help?

GORDON: It's no good asking them. They're lazy, that lot. I keep telling them, you know your trouble — you're bone idle. But they don't listen to me.

LEADER: Why?

GORDON: They've got mossy ears as well.

LEADER: Look, if you're all suffering from the same thing, you could help each other. You could do each others' ears. You could dust each others' backs.

GORDON: You say that, but I know what would happen. The others wouldn't pull their weight. It would be the cobwebs all over again.

LEADER: Cobwebs?

GORDON: Gary asked Griselda to help him get rid of cobwebs. So she did. But then when Griselda asked Gary to do the same thing he wouldn't help out. He said he was too busy. So now, no-one does anything for anyone. It's every gargoyle for himself up here, I can tell you.

LEADER: Well, that's no good, is it? Look at you – everyone refusing to help out and what happens? A load of dirty gargoyles with mossed-up ears. I know, Gordon, why don't you set an example? Why don't you start the ball rolling by helping out another gargoyle?

GORDON: Well, I could... it does get pretty annoying not being able to hear what people say. Yes, you're right. I'll help out. I'll deal with the moss.

LEADER: Then you'll be able to hear me more clearly.

GORDON: *(Pause)* On the other hand, there are some advantages to having blocked ears...

LEADER: Charming! *(To congregation)* See? That's what happens when no-one helps each other. I don't suppose any of you have moss in your ears. Well, not many of you anyway, but imagine what life would be like if people didn't do things for us? Imagine what our house or our workplaces or our churches would be like, if people didn't help out. What would life be like without volunteers – people who do things for us even though they're not paid? There would be few sports clubs. You might not have events to go to in your town or village. You probably wouldn't have a church.

So maybe it's time for us to give something back. And we'll start at home.

TakeAway: a chore chart

(See opposite for a blank chart)

*Ask people to fill in the chores that need doing down the left hand
column of the chore chart. Then put the names of family members
in the other columns as required. Put a list of suggested jobs on the
OHP or Powerpoint. You could include:*

▷ *Tidy your room*   ▷ *Help with the laundry*

▷ *Clear the table*   ▷ *Wash the car*

▷ *Cook the meal*   ▷ *Wash the dishes*

▷ *Make your bed*   ▷ *Mow the lawn...*

*Whatever you can think of! People should adapt the list to be as
specific as they can for their family.*

Prayer: thanks for those who serve us

Lord, we thank you for all the people who spend their lives as servants
not stars,

who serve us day by day.

We think of those who serve us in our homes, or who bring things to
our door; those who serve us in our shops, surgeries and hospitals, in
factories, in business,

people who affect our lives even though they will never meet us,

who may indeed live on the other side of the world.

We thank you for the people who make our clothes, grow our food,
build our cars, provide us with energy for light and heat, and enable
us to travel.

We thank you for the people who have made all the different
appliances we have in our homes, that do some of our chores for us.

We thank you for people who serve us by entertaining us and keep us
happy.

We pray for those who are unhappy or hard-pressed.

We pray for children who are carers and workers in the home because
their parents are disabled or dependent.

We pray for more support for them through the local church and
other agencies.

Lastly, we pray for our lives, that we may be imitators of God.

Amen

Closing prayer

As we clean and tidy, cook and wait on others,

may we serve them as if they were Christ our Lord, the King of Kings.

Amen

In this column list the chores	In these columns list the person responsible on each day					
CHORES	MONDAY	TUESDAY	WEDNESDAY	THURSDAY	FRIDAY	SATURDAY

Getting ready

A week (or more) before

Drama: tidy up your room!

- [ ] Allocate parts and rehearse

Daisy Daytime: Help! My son's a couch potato!

- [ ] Allocate parts and give background material for hotseating

Drama: Gordon's mossy ears

- [ ] Photocopy script

TakeAway: a chore chart

- [ ] Photocopy/design chore charts

An hour (or more) before

- [ ] Arrange seating and set

Drama: tidy up your room!

- [ ] Put props and costumes in place

Drama: Gordon's mossy ears

- [ ] Set-up for Gordon (microphone, statue, etc. as required)

TakeAway: a chore chart

- [ ] Put chore charts in place
- [ ] Have pens or pencils handy

Father, dear Father

5. FATHER, DEAR FATHER

Aim: To thank God for the love of dads and to inspire dads with God's love

Bible Passage: Luke 15.20–24; 1 John 4

1. Want it!

The purpose here is to
▷ hear what God is like as a father
▷ find out what other peoples' dads are like

We do this by asking people to
▷ stand and listen
▷ sit and talk

The tools we use are
▷ Stand up and listen: the father love of God
▷ Comment: learning from our dads
▷ PairTalk: what have our dads ever done for us?
▷ Game: competitive dad

2. Watch it!

The purpose here is to
▷ contrast earthly fathers with God the Father

We do this by asking people to
▷ watch a drama
▷ listen to the Bible

The tools we use are
▷ Drama: mud on the carpet
▷ Bible: Luke 15.20–24

3. Try it!

The purpose here is to
▷ recognise the importance of dads and give thanks for them

We do this by asking people to
▷ listen to Gordon
▷ pray

The tools we use are
▷ Drama: Gordon's dad (part 1)
▷ Prayer: thanks for dads
▷ Prayer: great-grandfather God

4. Live it!

The purpose here is to
▷ celebrate the relationship between dads and children

We do this by asking people to
▷ listen to a sermon extract
▷ pray
▷ listen to Gordon
▷ write a gift tag

The tools we use are
▷ Spurgeon's sermon
▷ Drama: Gordon's dad (part 2)
▷ TakeAway: some cable ties
▷ Closing prayer

Running order

When	What	Who
	Want it!	
	Stand up and listen: the father love of God	
	Comment: learning from our dads	
	PairTalk: what's your dad ever done for you?	
	Game: competitive dad	
	Watch it!	
	Drama: mud on the carpet	
	Bible: Luke 15.20–24	
	Try it!	
	Drama: Gordon's dad (part 1)	
	Prayers: thanks for dads and 'great grandfather God'	
	Live it!	
	Spurgeon's sermon: many kisses for returning sinners	
	Drama: Gordon's dad (part 2)	
	TakeAway: some cable ties	
	Closing prayer	

Want it!

LEADER: Welcome to our service, which today is all about fathers. So let's start by thinking about God our father.

Stand up and listen: the father love of God

Stand up everybody and listen.
Listen to what God is like:
He is the King,
but a humble king,[1]
patient and gentle,
faithful and wise.
He loves those who don't love him,
and those who are his enemies.[2]
He cares for those who are alone,
and is slow to become angry with all.[3]
He is generous,
and doesn't find fault.
He is wise,
and loves to give wisdom.[4]
He chooses his words carefully,
to refresh our spirits,
and wants all people to know that they can trust him.[5]
He rewards perseverance,
and is good through and through.[6]
Stand up everybody and listen:
this is what our God is like.

---

[1] *Zechariah 9.9;* [2] *Matthew 5.43;* [3] *Psalm 103.8;* [4] *James 1.5;* [5] *John 14.1;* [6] *James 1.12–13*

Comment: learning from our dads

LEADER: Today we'll be looking at a story that Jesus told about a father and a son, but first let's think about Jesus himself. He had two fathers really.

▷ Who were they?

Jesus obviously relied on his true father, God, but he also must have learned a lot from Joseph. Fathers in Jesus' day considered themselves responsible for three main things: teaching their sons a job, teaching them the law and finding them a good wife!

We know that Joseph taught Jesus his trade: that of a carpenter and builder. And we know that Jesus grew up with a knowledge of the law of God. He was able to quote Scripture to people who challenged him and even to the devil when tempted. But, despite what some modern novelists claim, I don't think Joseph found him a wife!

▷ What's your dad like?
▷ What's his job?
▷ What have you learned from him?
▷ Has he found you a wife yet?

PairTalk: what's your dad ever done for you?

Get feedback and compare peoples different experiences of learning from their fathers.

Bring fathers and children together in pairs/groups to compare what they said to others. They could do this privately or publicly.

Game: competitive dad

LEADER: Have you ever seen the character in *The Fast Show*, called 'Competitive Dad'?

You could show a clip to illustrate this point

He's got to be the best at everything. He torments his long-suffering children, Toby and Peter, with constant challenges they can never live up to.

Sport is Competitive Dad's greatest interest, from cricket to tennis and fishing, not to mention weight-lifting and Monopoly.

Simon Day – the actor who played the part – said that the character was inspired by a dad he saw one day at the swimming pool. He challenged his two young children to a race. Instead of giving them a chance, he haired off across the pool, then waited smugly for his struggling sprogs to catch up.

Has anybody got a dad like that?

Well, here's a chance for you to find out.

Invite two pairs of fathers and their (eldest) child up to the front. Stage a contest between father and child. It could be arm-wrestling, or 'Paper, Scissors, Stone' or similar. Make it simple, but competitive! If you want a game where the children have more chance of winning, you could always set up a games console and show it on a big screen or via the computer!

Encourage everyone to try their hardest and get the congregation to shout their support.

Once the game is over, ask dads and offspring:
  ▷ *How did you feel about winning/losing?*

LEADER: Sometimes dads try not to win because they don't want us to lose heart. But sometimes we want to know our fathers are stronger than us so that we can be proud of them. It's reassuring to know that your dad is strong, protective, clever.

And we want to know that they love us, whatever happens.

Watch it!

Drama: mud on the carpet

SEAN is looking anxiously out over the congregation, as if he is looking for someone. Then, from the back of the church, SHANE enters. He trudges wearily up to the front. He looks completely wrecked. His clothes are muddy and torn.

SEAN: *(Sympathetically)* Oh, son. I've been looking out for you. We saw all the television coverage. It looked awful. Why didn't you call?

SHANE: I didn't want to bother you.

SEAN: Don't be silly. I'd have come and picked you up.

SHANE: You wouldn't have got near the place. There were tractors stuck in the mud. And anyway... I thought you'd be mad at me.

SEAN: Mad? Why should I be mad?

SHANE: Well, look at me.

SEAN: Come on, Shane! It's not your fault that the festival was washed out. I mean who could predict a typhoon like that would happen. *(Pause)* In Berkshire. *(Pause)* In August.

SHANE: I lost the tent. It was completely flooded away. Ruined.

SEAN: It's just an old tent. Nothing special.

SHANE: And the sleeping bag. It was soaked.

SEAN: It's not your fault.

SHANE: Even your wellies got ruined.

SEAN: It doesn't matter. I'm glad you took them. I hate to think what would have happened without them. Now come and have a drink.

SHANE: It's good to be home.

He walks further onto the stage.

SHANE: Oh, I'm afraid I got a bit of mud on the carpet...

SEAN: Don't worry, it's not your... *(realising)* what did you say?

SHANE: I got a bit of mud on the carpet. Well, I'm sort of caked in it.

SEAN: *(Slowly)* Mud on the carpet. But that's new.

SHANE: *(Not realising that the mood is changing)* Yeah, well, anyway, I'm home now.

SEAN: Yes, you're home now, and apparently you're bringing the festival with you.

SHANE: But I thought you said it wasn't my fault...

SEAN: The festival wasn't your fault. The typhoon wasn't your fault. But the carpet's different. Do you know how much that new carpet cost?

SHANE: Wait a minute, wait a minute – why are you mad? You didn't worry about the tent or the sleeping bag...

SEAN: They were old, this is new. How could you be so irresponsible!

SHANE: I thought you were pleased to see me.

SEAN: That was before you decided to use my new carpet to recreate the landscape of the Somme. Look at it!

SHANE: It's not that bad!

SEAN: Not that bad! There's so much mud there, we might as well leave it and use it to grow potatoes.

SHANE: I've had a terrible weekend. I've had a terrible journey home and now all you care about is your rotten carpet! I'm going to my room!

He starts to go. He has almost left when SEAN speaks.

SEAN: *(Quietly)* Shane.

SHANE stops.

SEAN: Shane.

SHANE turns round, as if they are going to be reconciled.

SEAN: *(Shouting)* Take your flipping shoes off!

Exit

Bible: Luke 15.20–24

LEADER: What did you think of that? Did Sean react as you expected? Is that what you would do, or would expect your dad to do?

 ▷ What's the difference between the way the two fathers acted?

Jesus tells a story where a son comes home from a bad experience. But in his story the ending was a bit different.

 ▷ Was this dad bad? Mad? Sad? Or glad?

Read the Bible account in Luke 15.20–24.

You could use a board to display them. If possible, show them the picture of Rembrandt's 'The return of the prodigal son.' (See 'Might come in handy' p.77)

Try it!

Drama: Gordon's dad (part 1)

LEADER: God is our father, our perfect father. But some earthly fathers may not be as good...

GORDON: *(Sniffs)*

LEADER: Hello? Did you hear something, just then?

GORDON: *(Sniffs again, slight weeping)*

LEADER: Who is it? Is there someone next to you who's upset?

GORDON: *(Starts crying)*

LEADER: Who is it? *(Feels a splash, looks up)* Gordon, what's the matter?

GORDON: *(Sobs uncontrollably)* I can't bear it!

LEADER: Oh dear. Hang on a minute. I'll just get you a hankie, then you can tell me all about it. *(Asks congregation for a hankie)* How are we going to get it up to Gordon? We need a pole. *(LEADER puts hankie on pole up to Gordon. Gordon, rather explosively, blows his nose)* Is that better? Can you tell us now why you're crying?

GORDON: It's all this talk of dads. It makes me think of my dad!

LEADER: Where is he?

GORDON: He's a long way away. He got bought by a museum. And now he's part of an exhibit on early medieval stone carving!

LEADER: That doesn't sound too bad.

GORDON: In New York!

LEADER: Ah. Well, that is a bit of a long way away. Do you ever visit him?

GORDON: *(Suddenly not crying)* I'm a gargoyle. Have a bit of perspective. I can't exactly hop on a plane, can I?

LEADER: No, I suppose not.

GORDON: But I miss him. And I never got to say goodbye properly.

LEADER: Why was that?

GORDON: We argued a lot. I told him he was... stony-hearted.

LEADER: You had a rocky relationship.

GORDON: I'll do the puns, thank you. But you're right. And now I'll miss him. *(Wailing)* And I'll never get to see him again!

LEADER: There must be some way we could contact him.

Congregation suggest how Gordon and dad could be reconciled.

LEADER: I know — all museums have websites now. We could email him. What's the name of the museum where he is?

GORDON: The Dwight Wright Hackenfaffer Institute of Ostentatious Art. He's in the 'Medieval Ugliness' wing.

LEADER: I'll send an email straight away telling him you'd like to get in touch. I'm sure we can work something out. *(To congregation)* See? It's not easy being a dad. We should pray for fathers and their children, and ask God to protect them from the kind of arguments Gordon was talking about.

Prayer: thanks for dads

If their dad is there, each child should go and sit or stand by him and hold his hand. Ask them to repeat after you this simple prayer.

Dear Lord,

Thank you for my dad.

Thank you that he loves me.

Thank you that you love him, too.

Amen

Prayer: great grandfather God

LEADER: Great grandfather God, you who are a father to the fathers and grandfathers here, we pray for them, knowing that their love and interest has the power to shape and influence many lives.

We pray that as your sons they would look up to you, spend time with you, and that their values would reflect yours. Great scientist, artist, engineer, we pray that in their work they would recognise and have confidence in your wisdom and skill, and that they would lean on it and learn from you.

Great friend and constant companion, we pray that in their friendships they would be able to give and receive encouragement, support, honesty, forgiveness and laughter to enjoy the good times and to get through the difficult times.

We pray these things for all the dads here.

And we pray all these things for our church leaders *(name them...)*, as they nurture the family of God, here at *(name your church...)*

We pray for the elders of our community, and for those we know who are in positions of responsibility. We pray for those in the public eye, whose daily lives are scrutinised so closely. Help them, as children loved by you, to become like you.

Let's have a brief silence in which to think about dads who aren't here with us.

Silence

We pray for those who are not here because they live somewhere else. Bless them, Lord, and let them know they are loved.

We pray for those who are distant from us in other ways, too. Maybe we don't get on very well these days; we don't speak much.

We pray for your help in forgiving one another, reconciling fathers and sons, fathers and daughters.

We pray, lastly, for those dads who are no longer with us. We thank you for the memory of them and remember that we are the guardian of all the good things they've taught us.

Thank you, Lord.

Amen

Live it!

Spurgeon's Sermon: Many Kisses for Returning Sinners or Prodigal Love for the Prodigal Son

LEADER: Everyone has parent problems. I expect there are people here who have had unhappy experiences with their parents at one time or another.

Sometimes, it's not serious, it's just the kind of things we saw in the drama. But sometimes it is serious and it can get so bad that you want to leave home. Maybe you never take it that far – maybe you just make use of your parents – money, things you want, but you don't give them any love or respect. You don't want them getting in your way. But, in most cases they don't give up on us. In fact, they can't seem to stop loving us.

It's the same with God. He's our rightful father, but we live as if he doesn't exist. It's as if we've run away from him, thinking life will be better without him. But it isn't. It only gets better when we realise we need him and really enjoy living with him.

Look at Rembrandt's 'The return of the prodigal son' again.

Charles Haddon Spurgeon, who was a Baptist minister in the nineteenth century, preached a whole sermon on the moment in the story when the father welcomed his son back home with many kisses. It was called 'Many Kisses for Returning Sinners or Prodigal Love for the Prodigal Son.' They knew how to do sermon titles in those days!

If you're feeling particularly dramatic, you could have someone playing Spurgeon, climbing into the pulpit dressed in Victorian gear. (A big false beard might help.) You could also have a father and son standing somewhere else, in a bear hug, as a visual aid.

SPURGEON: You see, this kiss was before the family fellowship. Before the servants had prepared the meal, before there had been any music or dancing in the family, his father kissed him. The son would have cared little for all their songs, and have valued but slightly his reception by the servants, if, first of all, he had not been welcomed to his father's heart. So it is with us; we need first to have fellowship with God before we think much of union with His people.

Before I go to join a church, I want my Father's kiss. Before the pastor gives me the right hand of fellowship, I want my heavenly Father's right hand to welcome me. Before I become recognised by God's people here

below, I want a private recognition from the great Father above; and that
He gives to all who come to Him as the prodigal came to his father. May
He give to some of you now!

LEADER: Thank you. Let's be quiet now and receive that private recognition
from the great Father above, the kiss of God toward us prodigals, wel-
coming us here.

Allow time for a moment of silent prayer.

Drama: Gordon's dad (part 2)

---

*After a sufficient pause, someone runs in from the back with a mes-
sage. He gives it to the LEADER.*

LEADER: Gordon! It's an email from your dad!

GORDON: From Dad?

LEADER: Shall I read it out?

GORDON: I would. Otherwise it lacks a certain dramatic effect.

LEADER: Quite. Well, it reads:

Dear Gordon,

Great to hear from you after all these years – we haven't spoken for such
a long time. I've been thinking about you a lot over here. But I have
some good news. I'm coming back as part of a touring exhibition! If you
can get someone to pick me up, I'd love to come and visit you.

Lots of love,

Dad

LEADER: You see? What did I tell you?

GORDON: Pick him up! That's typical of him. He weighs a ton. I don't know.
He just emails out of the blue and expects me to do all the arrange-
ments. That's typical!

LEADER: Some people – some gargoyles – are never happy.

TakeAway – some cable ties

---

*Buy enough packets of cable ties for all the fathers in church, and
some extra for children to take home to their dads.*

LEADER: On Mother's Day we give all the mums some flowers. But what do
you give your dad on Father's Day?

We've proved that dads are useful for all sorts of things, this morning!
They love mending things, they love DIY! So we have something that will
be useful in every household: some cable ties!

Your dad will really thank you for these. No, really. And if you throw a
Screwfix catalogue in, he'll be ecstatic. You just need to write on the gift
tag now.

Prepare some gift tags with the following verse on. Or, if there's time, let people write this on their gift tag in their own hand.

'Love is more important than anything else. It is what ties everything completely together. Colossians 3.14'

Closing prayer

Lord, this morning, you have reminded us that love is
more important than anything else.
It is what ties everything completely together.
We need our dads' love.
And we need you.
We need the warmth of your love,
like the warmth of being at home.
We try to live without you,
and then we become afraid,
worrying what you will say,
wondering if you still like us.
We needn't worry.
You are always looking out for us,
even when we're far away,
waiting to welcome us home.
Thank you, Lord.
We want to love like you.
Amen

Might come in handy

At the end of the service you could play the song from the *Lion King*: 'He lives in you'. Or you could have a special Father's Day showing of *Lion King* or *The Railway Children* or *Finding Nemo* or any other film that celebrates dads. Or for a kind of 'Prodigal Son in reverse' you could show the clip from *The Railway Children* when the father comes home to the children after being in prison.

About the picture

Rembrandt's 'The return of the prodigal son' is available from:

www.lds.org/ch/rembrandt/exhibit.html etching

The painting is at the archive website or from the website of the Hermitage in St Petersburg.

About Charles Haddon Spurgeon

Born in Kelvedon, Essex, Spurgeon was converted to Christianity on January 6, 1850 at the age of fifteen. He preached his first sermon in 1851 and was ordained as pastor of the small Baptist church at Waterbeach, Cambridgeshire two years later. A year after that, aged just 19, he was called to the famous New Park Street Chapel, Southwark, the largest Baptist congregation in London at the time. Within a few months of Spurgeon's arrival at Park Street, his powers as a preacher made him famous. By the time of his death in 1892, he had preached well over 3,500 sermons and published forty-nine books.

He was a controversial figure, often attacked in the media, and embroiled in theological disputes. However, the popularity of his preaching was only too obvious. In venues such as the Surrey Music Hall he preached to audiences numbering more than ten thousand – and not a microphone to be seen!

On October 7, 1857 he preached to the largest crowd ever: 23,654 people at The Crystal Palace in London. In 1861 the congregation moved permanently to the newly constructed purpose-built Metropolitan Tabernacle at Elephant and Castle, Southwark, seating five thousand people with standing room for another thousand.

About Father's Day

Father's Day is a relatively modern celebration, beginning in 1908 in the United States. Reputedly the inspiration behind the day was a deadly mine explosion which killed 361 men, many of them fathers. Another – more likely – explanation is that Mother's Day was very popular and fathers wanted to get in on the act. It gained support from American presidents and has now spread throughout the world.

About cable ties

We got this idea from a friend of ours who said that when he gave these out at his church one Father's Day they were incredibly popular. No, really.

Getting ready

Week (or more) before

PairTalk: what have our dads ever done for us?

☐ Put questions on Powerpoint

Game: competitive dad

☐ Prepare anything needed for game

☐ Get *Fast Show* clip if possible

Drama: mud on the carpet

☐ Allocate parts and rehearse

Drama: Gordon's dad (part 1 and 2)

☐ Photocopy parts

Spurgeon's sermon

☐ Allocate part and get costume organised

TakeAway: cable ties

☐ Buy a load of cable ties

An hour (or more) before

☐ Arrange seating and set

☐ Check AV resources (*Fast Show* clip and *Return of the Prodigal Son* picture)

Drama: mud on the carpet

☐ Put props and costumes in place

Drama: Gordon's dad (part 1 and 2)

☐ Set-up for Gordon (microphone, statue, etc. as required)

Spurgeon's sermon

☐ Put costume in place

Family

Best of
friends

6. BEST OF FRIENDS

Aim: To show what kind of a friend Jesus is and to see what kind of friend he wants us to be

Bible Passage: Luke 19.1–10

1. Want it!

The purpose here is to
▷ introduce the subject of friendship

We do this by asking people to
▷ spot the difference in a picture
▷ listen

The tools we use are
▷ Quiz: spot the difference
▷ Stand up and listen: God the friend
▷ Drama: Gordon's grump

2. Watch it!

The purpose here is to
▷ find out what kind of friendship Jesus showed

We do this by asking people to
▷ listen to the Bible
▷ correct the errors

The tools we use are
▷ Bible: Luke 19.1–10 with deliberate mistakes
▷ Comment: spot the difference

3. Try it!

The purpose here is to
▷ try out ways of showing friendship

We do this by asking people to
▷ question the characters in the Bible story
▷ pray about being a good friend

The tools we use are
▷ Daisy Daytime: Help! My leader wants me to be friends with a short tax-collector!
▷ Moving prayer: you've got a friend

4. Live it!

The purpose here is to
▷ think how to make a difference this week

We do this by asking people to
▷ listen
▷ pray
▷ take two sweets

The tools we use are
▷ Comment: spot the difference in you
▷ TakeAway: two friendship sweets
▷ Closing prayer

Running order

When	What	Who
	Want it!	
	Quiz: spot the difference	
	Stand up and listen: God the Friend	
	Drama: Gordon's grump	
	Watch it!	
	Bible: Luke 19.1–10 with deliberate mistakes	
	Comment: spot the difference	
	Try it!	
	Daisy Daytime: Help! My leader wants me to be friends with a short tax-collector!	
	Moving prayer: you've got a friend	
	Live it!	
	Comment: spot the difference in you	
	TakeAway: two friendship sweets	
	Closing prayer	

Want it!

LEADER: Welcome to our service this morning which is all about friends.

Stand up and listen: God the friend

Stand up everybody and listen,
Listen to what our God is like:
He is the creator of this vast universe;[1]
we are in awe, he deserves our respect,
but he is also beside us as a friend.
The Bible records how he has drawn close to people,
as close as the breath we draw.
He confided in Abraham [2]
and spoke face to face with Moses.[3]
He is the friend who loves at all times,
who sticks closer than a brother.[4]
Jesus was happy to be called the friend of outcasts,
tax-collectors and 'sinners.'[5]
He is the friend that we know we can call on at midnight,
knocking on his door for help in an emergency.[6]
He laid down his life for his friends.[7]

---

[1] *Genesis 1.1;* [2] *Genesis 18.17;* [3] *Exodus 33.9;* [4] *Proverbs 18.24;*
[5] *Matthew 11.19;* [6] *Luke 11.5–8;* [7] *John 15.13*

Quiz: spot the difference

Before the service, find a spot the difference puzzle which you can show on PowerPoint or copy onto paper.

LEADER: I want you to look at the two pictures. How many differences can you spot?

Give people time to spot all the differences.

Gordon's grump

GORDON: Excuse me!

LEADER: Gordon? Is that you? You're awake a bit early today, aren't you?

GORDON: I just need to be sure about something, that's all. You're not going to do any of this 'talking in pairs' business, today, are you?

LEADER: Why not?

GORDON: It's just I always have to talk to Griselda.

LEADER: Who is Griselda?

GORDON: She's another gargoyle.

LEADER: What's the problem with talking to her?

GORDON: She's really uncool. She still thinks wearing moss is fashionable. And she talks funny. All of us other gargoyles, we don't like her.

LEADER: Gordon! That's not a very nice thing to say.

GORDON: Well, it's true. And anyway, she's not the same as us. *(Whispers)* Gregory says that she's not made out of the same stone as the rest of us. She might be sandstone. Or even gypsum.

LEADER: What does that matter? Don't you like other gargoyles?

GORDON: Of course I like other gargoyles. I like them as long as they're like me. And she's very bad-tempered. She got really angry the other day, just because we wouldn't let her join in our game of Elgin Marbles.

LEADER: Perhaps you should have let her join in.

GORDON: Oh, it was only a joke. She's got no sense of humour.

LEADER: I think you need to listen to this service carefully and change your attitude, young man.

GORDON: Young man? I'm six hundred years old.

LEADER: Well, act your age then. Because our service today is all about friendship. Watch it!

Bible: Luke 19.1–10 with deliberate mistakes

LEADER: We're going to hear a story from the Bible. But like that picture at the beginning, this version has some things that are different. So, listen carefully and tell me, what's wrong with this Bible version?

READER: Jesus was going through Jericho, where a man named Zacchaeus lived. He was in charge of collecting taxes and was very rich.

Jesus was heading his way, and Zacchaeus wanted to see what he was like. But Zacchaeus was a short man and could not see over the crowd. So he ran ahead and climbed up into a sycamore tree.

When Jesus got there, he looked up and said,

'Zacchaeus, what on earth are you doing up that tree? You look ridiculous! Come down at once, you're making a complete fool of yourself in front of all these people!'

So Zacchaeus came down from the tree immediately, feeling even smaller than he already was, and pleaded with Jesus to come round to his house after all, all the time apologising to Jesus for embarrassing him in public.[1]

'Alright then,' Jesus said. 'Normally I wouldn't go anywhere near someone like you, but as you've got a lot of dosh and I need a good meal, I might be persuaded.'[2]

Everyone who saw this started grumbling, 'This man Zaccheus is a sinner! And Jesus is going home to eat with him.'

When Jesus heard this, he said to Zaccheus, 'I've changed my mind. I've heard the rumours about you and I think I'd best cancel my visit. After all, I've got my reputation to think of.'[3]

Later that day, Zacchaeus stood up and said to the Lord, 'I will give half of my property to the poor, and I will now pay back four times as much to everyone I have ever cheated.'

Jesus said to Zaccheus,

'Don't think you can get away with it that easily. In your job as a tax collector, you've charged ordinary people far too much tax – in fact, you are a thief and a robber. You ought to be punished. Saying that you will give away some of your money to the poor, is just a ploy to try and salve your guilty conscience and get yourself off the hook. You are a son of Abraham, a Jewish citizen, and the sooner you are punished for your crimes the better. I have come to this world to point out people's wrongdoings and make sure they are properly punished for them.'[4]

Comment: spot the difference

LEADER: There were some things wrong with that version of the story! Can you help me spot what they were? Open your Bibles at Luke 19.1-10. Listen again and imagine you have a buzzer button in front of you.

Practice making a buzzer sound.

Whenever you hear anything that sounds wrong, press your imaginary buzzer.

Start reading again and stop when people buzz.

Identify what's wrong. Re-read the correct version.

Then recap, linking in with the numbers in the passage above.

1. Jesus didn't criticise

When Jesus got there, he didn't criticise or mock Zacchaeus for climbing a tree. He said, 'Zacchaeus hurry down! I want to stay with you today' (Lk. 19.5). Zacchaeus hurried down and gladly welcomed Jesus.

2. Jesus wasn't in it for himself

He didn't invite himself to Zacchaeus' house just because he needed a meal, or because Zacchaeus was rich. He was prepared to befriend him regardless of his reputation.

3. Jesus didn't listen to gossip or rumour

Although Luke says 'Everyone who saw this started grumbling, "This man Zacchaeus is a sinner! And Jesus is going home to eat with him"' (Lk. 19.7), Jesus took no notice.

4. Jesus forgave Zacchaeus and saw what he could be

He said to Zacchaeus, 'Today you and your family have been saved, because you are a true son of Abraham. The Son of Man came to look for and to save people who are lost' (Lk. 19.9).

In all of this Jesus shows extraordinary friendship. But I wonder if other people – those who were there at the time – saw it like that.

Try it!

Daisy Daytime: Help! My leader wants me to be friends with a short tax-collector!

Enter Daisy Daytime. She introduces the title of the show and brings out the Disciple first.

?
Questions for Disciple
▷ What's a disciple? Who do you follow?
▷ What has he asked you to do?
▷ Why shouldn't you be friends with a tax collector?
▷ Why don't you give up being his disciple?

The Disciple could give us more details:

▷ *Jesus keeps spending time with the wrong sort of people. He even goes to parties with them!*

▷ *Everyone knows tax-collectors collaborate with the Romans.*

▷ *He wants to follow Jesus, but Jesus makes all these demands.*

Then Daisy introduces Zacchaeus.

?
Questions for Zacchaeus
▷ Why doesn't anyone like you?
▷ Why do you insist on climbing trees?
▷ What difference does it make to be noticed by Jesus?

Zacchaeus could give us more details:

▷ *Just because he's a tax-collector doesn't mean he's all bad.*

▷ *He climbed the tree because he was desperate to get to Jesus.*

▷ *He's going to change, because of the love Jesus showed him.*

?
Questions for both of them
▷ What do you think Jesus means by all this?
▷ How does he expect his followers to behave?

DAISY: Well, that's all we have time for. On the bad side, we've seen how short tax-collectors can rip people off and make them angry. But on the good side, I've been able to get some help filling in my tax return. You've been watching the Daisy Daytime show. Goodbye, and, remember, never go swimming immediately after a big meal.

Daisy and the other characters exit.

Moving prayer: you've got a friend

LEADER: Who did you sympathise with? With Zacchaeus? With the Disciple?

OK, you've been sitting still and listening for long enough.

I want everyone to get up and spread out. Find a place to stand or sit on your own for a moment.

Everyone moves to a place on their own.

We've probably all known times when we've felt as if we had no friends, no-one to sit with, no-one to share things with.

Can you think of a time when you've felt like that? You've watched everyone else having a good time, but you don't feel at the centre of things. It's not a nice feeling.

What's worse is we sometimes make other people feel like that.

We're going to pray, and I'd like you to put your hands over your face.

VOICE 1: We're sorry, Lord Jesus, when we've not been a good friend to others.

We remember in silence the things we're ashamed to say out loud.

Pause

You know that we want to appear 'in' with those who are popular,

we're afraid to be friends with certain people,

we worry what others will think,

and so we overlook those who are not like us,

or we join in the gossip and knock our friends down.

Sometimes our families are the last people we make friends with,

we forget that they need our friendship too.

Lord, be our friend, and forgive us these things.

Amen

LEADER: Now, I want you to get together in groups of four or five. You can sit or stand.

Everyone moves into groups.

When we're with friends, we feel happy, attractive, popular.

We have lots to talk about, lots to do and lots to take our minds off ourselves.

I want you to stand in a huddle, arms on each others' shoulders. Let's pray.

VOICE 2: Thank you, Father, for our friends:
  let's think of their names in the silence now.

Pause

For the ones we have a laugh with,
who make us feel that we're never alone,
for those who accept us as we are, not for what we've got,
who tell us the truth, but forgive us our weaknesses,
who stick by us when things go wrong.
They are a gift from you and show us what you are like.
Lord, be our friend, too, and help us to be good friends like you.
Amen

LEADER: When we're surrounded by friends, we may not notice how other
  people – who are not part of the group – are feeling. Or if we do, we
  don't do anything about it. We could, but it's safer and easier not to.
  But no-one should have to be on their own, especially not in a church.
  So let's now sit down all together.

Everyone returns to their seats.

Close up the gaps, no-one sitting on their own. Let's see if we can do it.
And now let's link arms or hold hands so that the whole church is joined
up, and let's pray one more time.

Everyone gets closer together and joins hands or links arms.

VOICE 3: Lord, we want to be friends with people here, at home, at school,
  at work, and where we live.
  So here we are, Lord, ready to start again.
  We think now of those we know, who want or need our friendship.

Pause

Holy Spirit, show us what we can do to make the first move,
to make them feel that they belong.
Help us to speak up for them when they're being put down,
to see what they need and share what we've got.
With the courage and love that you give us,
help us to make a difference to someone this week and be a friend to
them.
Amen

Live it!

Comment: spot the difference in you

LEADER: If we are followers of Jesus, we can't listen to his words and then ignore them.

In the Bible, James says this:

'Obey God's message! Don't fool yourselves by just listening to it. If you hear the message and don't obey it, you are like people who stare at themselves in a mirror and forget what they look like as soon as they leave. But you must never stop looking at the perfect law that sets you free. God will bless you in everything you do, if you listen and obey, and don't just hear and forget.' (Jas. 1.22–25)

Imagine looking in the mirror and then forgetting what we look like the minute we walk away! No, you remember what you look like, don't you? Well, remember what Jesus wants you to be like.

Next time you see someone who could do with a friendly hello, or who is sitting on their own, remember what Jesus would do. Remember what we did today in church and keep putting it into practice this week. If you are a disciple of Jesus, people should be able to spot the difference in you. You don't go with the crowd necessarily, you think for yourself and you offer respect and friendship to all, as Jesus would.

Maybe last week you wouldn't have done this, but now you know, and there's no getting away from it. It's like spot the difference. Last week you weren't always a friend to everyone, this week you are a friend to everyone; last week you didn't share, this week you do share. Spot the difference. I'll show you what I mean.

TakeAway: two friendship sweets

Use two volunteers (A and B) as visual aids. Give each person in the congregation two (wrapped) sweets each.

LEADER: Here are two sweets. One sweet is for you, and the other is for someone else.

A offers sweet to B.

They are to be eaten together with someone this week.

You don't eat one now and then save the other to give away at some other time.

A mimes eating sweet on their own first, goes off, then comes back on gives sweet to B and watches him eat it.

You don't give it to someone and then walk away.

A gives sweet to B and walks away without saying anything.

Instead you talk to them and share a conversation as well as your sweets.

> *A says to B: 'Hi, how are you? Would you like a sweet? These are my favourites? What's your favourite?', etc.*

You consider people's feelings. You don't insult them. Don't say

> *A to B 'Hi, you look lonely and sad and we were told at church on Sunday to be nice to sad, lonely people. Would you like a sweet? No, don't thank me. I'm only obeying orders.'*

You just be as friendly as you can, the same as you would be with your other friends.

Do you think you can do this? We may need God's help on this, so let's finish with a prayer.

Closing prayer

Lord, help me to share and be a friend to others this week.

I might need to be brave, so please help me, even if others laugh at me or look down on me.

I'll need to listen to your voice, to obey you, so help me to be sensitive to you.

I want people to spot the difference in me so that, even without stepping foot inside this church, they realise what you are really like.

Amen

Might come in handy

About Zacchaeus

Apart from the passage in Luke 19.1–10, Zacchaeus is otherwise unknown. The name is the Greek version of the Hebrew name Zakkai or Zaccai which, ironically perhaps, means 'clean' or 'innocent.'

Later ecclesiastical tradition claims that Zacchaeus became Bishop of Caesarea, but there is no evidence of this.

Zacchaeus is designated 'chief tax collector' (Lk. 19.2). He would have been a supervisory official, probably with a number of employees collecting taxes for him. Jericho was a good city for a tax-collector, since it was an important customs station for the major trade route between Judea and the lands east of the Jordan. As a chief tax collector he was viewed by his fellow towns-people as an unclean sinner. The text does not explicitly say that he cheated anyone, but his response to Jesus may indicate that he felt guilty.

About tax-collectors

Direct taxes, such as taxes on individuals and land, were handled by the local government, either the Romans or whoever the Romans had put in charge.

But the right to collect indirect taxes – such as tolls or duties charged on goods being transported – were sold to the highest individual bidder. These tax collectors guaranteed to pay the government a certain sum, prior to collection. In order to make a profit, therefore, they had to collect as much as they could over and above that sum. So there was a huge incentive for the tax collectors to charge as much as they could, since they would keep the difference. This is why, when John preaches to them (Lk. 3.12–13), he tells them to collect no more than is 'allowed.'

It is worth remembering that the Jewish worker of the time not only had to pay imperial taxes, but also had to pay an annual temple tax and was subject to tithes on produce for the Jerusalem priests. So the tax burden was probably quite large and the tax-collectors were obvious targets for ill-feeling. Another reason they were disliked is that they were seen as 'collaborating' with the occupying power.

In fact, this distaste for tax-collectors was also enshrined in the religious laws. A section in the Mishnah – a collection of rabbinic law – says 'If a tax-gatherer enter a house, [all that is within] the house becomes unclean'.

Getting ready

A week (or more) before

Quiz: spot the difference

☐ Find 'spot the difference' puzzle and photocopy or put on Powerpoint

Drama: Gordon's grump

☐ Photocopy script

Daisy Daytime: Help! My leader wants me to be friends with a short tax-collector!

☐ allocate parts and give background material for hotseating

Moving prayer: you've got a friend

☐ Find three voices for the prayers

TakeAway : two friendship sweets

☐ Buy sweets

An hour (or more) before

☐ Arrange seating and set

Gordon's grump

☐ Set-up for Gordon (microphone, statue, etc. as required)

TakeAway : two friendship sweets

☐ Put sweets in place

Monday morning blues

7. MONDAY MORNING BLUES

Aim: To find the joy of work and school!

Bible: Ephesians 6.5–9

1. Want it!

The purpose here is to
▷ be inspired by God's work
▷ find out people's work

We do this by asking people to
▷ listen to what God is like as a worker
▷ guess what certain people do for a living
▷ talk to someone about their work

The tools we use are
▷ Stand up and listen: God the worker
▷ PairTalk: where are you on Monday morning?
▷ Game: what's my line?
▷ Interviews: work and God

2. Watch it!

The purpose here is to
▷ find out what kind of workers God wants us to be

We do this by asking people to
▷ watch drama
▷ listen to the Bible

The tools we use are
▷ Drama: Sherrill's new job
▷ Bible: Ephesians 6.5–9

3. Try it!

The purpose here is to
▷ encourage one another in our work
▷ see how we measure up to God's expectations

We do this by asking people to
▷ listen to Gordon
▷ talk about highs and lows of work

The tools we use are
▷ Drama: Gordon's Monday morning blues
▷ Prayertalk: off the record
▷ Prayer: God of our weekdays

4. Live it!

The purpose here is to
▷ help people remain inspired by God when they're at work tomorrow

We do this by asking people to
▷ pray for one another
▷ write memo to self
▷ write/draw on group picture

The tools we use are
▷ TakeAway: a memo to yourself
▷ Meditation: it's in the post!
▷ Closing prayer
▷ Display: where's the church on Monday morning?

Running order

When	What	Who
	Want it!	
	Stand up and listen: God the w/orker	
	PairTalk: where are you on a Monday morning?	
	Game: what's my line?	
	Interviews: work and God	
	Watch it!	
	Drama: Sherrill's new job	
	Bible: Ephesians 6.5–9	
	Try it!	
	Drama: Gordon's Monday morning blues	
	Prayertalk: off the record	
	Prayer: God of our weekdays	
	Live it!	
	TakeAway: a memo to yourself	
	Meditation: it's in the post!	
	Closing Prayer	
	Display: where is the church on Monday morning?	

Want it!

LEADER: Good morning. Welcome to today's Sunday morning service in which we will be thinking about what happens the rest of the week!

> **?** ▷ Who likes getting up at the weekend?
>   ▷ Who likes getting up on Monday morning?
>   ▷ Why is that?

LEADER: Well, let's enjoy the time we have now together in the presence of God, to find new inspiration for what we do in our daily lives and to pray for one another in the week ahead.

What does God do Monday to Friday? Do you think he enjoys his work?

Stand up and listen: God the worker

Stand up everybody and listen.
Listen to what our God is like.
From the beginning, Wisdom was with the Lord,
before he created the earth,
helping him to plan and to build.[1]
And now every day, the heavens declare the glory of God,
and the skies proclaim the work of his hands.[2]
Do you know what else our God has done?
Fearsome, extraordinary things,
written in the pages of the Bible.
They are part of our history.
And he has planned for us to do good things,
to live as he has always wanted us to live.
We are his workmanship.[3]
We know that God is always at work for the good
of everyone who loves him.[4]
Each generation will announce to the next
his wonderful and powerful deeds![5]

[1] *Proverbs 8.22–30;* [2] *Psalm19.1;* [3] *Ephesians 2.10;* [4] *Romans 8.28;*
[5] *Psalm 145.4*

PairTalk: where are you on Monday morning?

Mix people up so they talk to someone they don't know very well.

> **?** ▷ What do you do on a Monday?
>   ▷ Do you look forward to Monday mornings? Why/why not?

Game: what's my line?

This game is based on the well-known game in which contestants with unusual occupations sign in, perform a mime of the job that they do, then field yes-or-no questions from four panelists aiming to work out the contestant's job.

You need a host, a panel of four, and three contestants with interesting occupations.

The host introduces the first member of the panel, then they introduce the next panelist and so on.

At the beginning of a round, the contestant is asked to 'Enter and sign in, please.' The contestant writes their name on a small whiteboard. They are asked to perform a mime of the job that they do.

A panel of four does the guessing on behalf of the congregation.

Panelists take it in turn to ask yes/no questions. They can keep going as long as they get 'yes' as an answer, but if they get a 'No' then play passes on to the next panelist.

Panelists can voluntarily pass questioning on to the next person if they can't think what to ask. After ten 'No's questioning has to stop.

Interviews: work and God

Once the quizzing is over, try and make time to ask the contestant a little more about their work. Here are some basic questions to ask:

▷ Where do you work?
▷ What do you do?
▷ What hours do you do?
▷ How long have you been doing this job?
▷ What qualifications or experience equipped you for this job?

You can also use the following questions to find out how they feel their work expresses their faith in God:

▷ Why do you do this job?
▷ Were you aware of God leading you into this work? Or do you have a sense of God wanting you to be in this particular job?
▷ Does being a Christian make a difference to how this job is done?
▷ Is it ever difficult to be a Christian and do this job?

Tell people that at the end of the service you would like them all to write or draw something on a large sheet of paper which shows what they do on a Monday morning. Then they sign it.

Watch it!

Drama: Sherrill's new job

SHEILA is sitting reading Hello *magazine, as normal. Enter SHERRILL.*

SHEILA: Hello, love, how did you get on? How did it go?

SHERRILL: Oh, all right. What's for tea?

SHEILA: Well?

SHERRILL: Well, what?

SHEILA: Your first day. How did you get on?

SHERRILL: Oh, you know. I don't know if it's really me.

SHEILA: What do you mean? You've been looking for ages for a good holiday job.

SHERRILL: Yes, but I've got to think more long-term. Is it developing my skills properly? Is it a viable part of my career development?

SHEILA stares at SHERRILL for a moment.

SHEILA: It's a cleaning job.

SHERRILL: Exactly. That's the problem. I don't have the skills, really.

SHEILA: You're telling me.

SHERRILL: I mean, they got me there under false pretences. I had to do all this hoovering and washing and dusting. What's that all about, eh?

SHEILA: It's *cleaning*. You went for a job as a *cleaner*. The clue was in the title.

SHERRILL: I thought it would be, you know, more administrative.

SHEILA: Administrative? What planet are you on? I did wonder. I thought it didn't sound like your cup of tea.

SHERRILL: Yes, and you're right. First thing that happened when I got there, they gave me this enormous hoover, showed me where to switch it on and told me to get on with it. I ask you. Call that induction? Where's health and safety when you really need them?

SHEILA: Anyway, it's just for the holiday. I'm sure you'll get used to it.

SHERRILL: Ah, well, I don't know about that.

SHEILA: Oh, tell me you haven't given in your notice.

SHERRILL: No, no, no, nothing like that.

SHEILA: What, then?

SHERRILL: I got sacked.

SHEILA: Sacked!

SHERRILL: It wasn't my fault! I told them I wasn't suited to manual labour. And anyway, I got injured. Look – I cracked one of my nails.

SHEILA: You know your trouble? You want everything to be cushy. Everything to be easy. You hate the thought of doing stuff you don't like. If you don't want to do it, you don't do it.

SHERRILL: Well, why should I?

SHEILA: It's called work, Sherrill. They pay you for doing it because no-one would do it unless they got paid. And you have to learn that.

SHERRILL: But why can't I just do what I love doing for a living?

SHEILA: Because there's no such job as 'lying around on the sofa watching kids' TV and picking your toenails.' Look, every job is a mixture. Every job has stuff you enjoy doing and stuff you don't. You have to learn to deal with it. Why don't you ring the people up and see if you can get your job back?

SHERRILL: No need. I've got another job lined up already.

SHEILA: You have?

SHERRILL: Yeah, the local pool is looking for lifeguards. In fact *(looking at watch)* I'm just off for an interview.

SHERRILL exits. SHEILA thinks for a moment.

SHEILA: *(calling after SHERRILL)* But... but... you can't swim!

SHEILA exits.

Bible: Ephesians 6.5–9

LEADER: I don't know what you thought of Sherrill's attitude there. Maybe you agree with her point of view: why should we do what we don't want to do? Or maybe you think she's being utterly unrealistic. What should be our attitude to work?

In the Roman world the workforce were largely slaves. There were millions of slaves. Paul wrote some advice for slaves who had become Christians on what their attitude should be like. Here is Paul's letter to the workers:

Read Ephesians 6.5–9

 ▷ How is Paul telling the workers to behave?

LEADER: Paul tells slaves to respect their masters and to be loyal to them.

He says that they should work with integrity – doing the right thing even when no-one is watching.

He says an incredible thing: that slaves should work as if they were working for the Lord himself.

But it's not all one-way traffic. Masters are told to respect their slaves as well, and not to bully them or treat them with favouritism, because their real master is Jesus.

I wonder what our attitude to work would be like if we were working for Jesus?

Try it!

Gordon's Monday morning blues

GORDON: Can't we change the subject?

LEADER: Oh, it's Gordon. What's the matter?

GORDON: I don't like this subject. Can't we talk about something nice? I don't want to talk about work.

LEADER: Well, don't you think it's important? I mean, all these people here have to go to school or work tomorrow.

GORDON: I don't like Monday mornings. I don't like my work.

LEADER: Why not?

GORDON: It's not what you'd call fulfilling is it? All I do is hang on the wall all day. And I've been doing it quite a long time. Four centuries is a long time to be in one job.

LEADER: I suppose it is. Aren't you due for retirement?

GORDON: Not for another 347 years. At the moment I have to do what Godfrey says.

LEADER: Who's Godfrey?

GORDON: Godfrey's the Chief Gargoyle. He's supposed to be in charge of all of the gargoyles here. He bosses us about.'Do this, don't do that.' And he gives us homework.

LEADER: Homework?

GORDON: We're supposed to get our GCSE's – Gargoyle Certificate of Sculptural Education. Last night I had to do an essay on 'The role and significance of beards in late medieval gargoyle sculpture.' Next week we've got an exam in 'Advanced moss management for mature sculptures.' And I've got my appraisal tomorrow. You know, when your boss sits down with you and tells you what's wrong with you. It's like parents' evening, only without the parents. And not in the evening.

LEADER: Maybe it will be good. Maybe you'll find out things that could help you to be a better gargoyle.

GORDON: It won't. I've never learnt anything useful before. Although that's mainly because I never listen to him anyway.

LEADER: But he's your boss!

GORDON: Yeah, but what makes him so special? Just because he's a couple of centuries older than the rest of us, he thinks he can order us about. And he only got promoted because our last boss, Greville got dry rot in his mortar and fell off the wall.

LEADER: Well, anyway, perhaps you should give him a chance. He is your boss, after all.

GORDON: Rubbish. Down with all of them, that's what I say. I think we should all rebel. Gargoyles of the world unite – you have nothing to lose but your moss!

Prayertalk: off the record

LEADER: Generally, there always comes a point at work or school when you get to talk to someone about how you're getting on: your teacher, your boss or someone you work with. Gordon's got his appraisal tomorrow with his boss, Godfrey. I wonder what Godfrey will say?

 ▷ How would you appraise Gordon?

LEADER: What are Gordon's strengths and weaknesses?

Well, he's very stable. He's able to rise above things and get a different perspective on them.

But maybe his weaknesses are that he's a bit old. Not to mention inflexible.

Sometimes it can be helpful to talk to someone who doesn't work with you. They can ask useful questions, or just listen while you sound off.

Here's your chance now to have your say and for someone to listen, someone whom you don't see on a Monday morning, but who could pray for you in your work this week and then ask you how it's going when you see each other again.

Those of you who learn spellings at school know there's four parts to the process: look, cover, write, check.

Once we've all got into pairs I'm going to ask you to do four things: talk, listen, pray, check.

Ask one another questions like these and then read the Bible verse and prayer together. Then next week check up on each other.

▷ What makes you fed up, cross or lazy at school/work?
▷ What makes you get excited, and makes you work hard?
▷ What are you like? If someone were to shadow you for the day, what would they think of you?
▷ What help do you need from the Lord for this week?

For very young ones who can't answer such questions, ask them to draw a picture of themselves at playgroup or wherever they are on a Monday morning.

LEADER: Let's read together: Isaiah 41.13

'I am the Lord your God.

I am holding your hand,

so don't be afraid.

I am here to help you.'

Lord, please help us all this week.

Amen

Prayer: God of our weekdays

God of our weekdays,
We pray to you about our Monday to Friday lives.
We ask you to work alongside us.
Help us to make the right decisions,
Help us to learn from others,
Help us to serve our colleagues, customers or clients with joy and patience.

God of our weekdays
We pray to you about those who have no work.
We ask you to be with them in their search.
Help them to find work that is fulfilling,
Help them to find work that gives them the money they need,
Help them to have confidence in themselves,
Help them to see that they are loved and valued by you.

God of our weekdays
We pray to you about people who struggle with work.
We ask you to change their situation.
Help them to see what is good in their task.
Help them to enjoy what they do.
Help them to find a way forward.
Help them to see you at work in their situation.
Help them to find help.

Amen

Live it!

TakeAway: a memo to yourself

LEADER: We all have to do things during the week that we find difficult or tiring or unenjoyable.

We also, I hope, have aspects of our jobs or education that we really enjoy. So what does God want you to be like this week? How does he want you to act in your school or workplace?

I wonder if you get memos at your work? A memo is sent round to people to remind them of something or announce something important. (Or sometimes, not so important!)

But what I want us to do is write a memo to ourselves this week. Maybe you could write on it something you've learnt today about work, or maybe you could remind yourself of what God wants you to be like.

Give people memos. See p.104 for a photocopiable memo sheet.
Or you can copy the headings and make your own. These could be
printed on the service sheet or given out as separate sheets of paper.
Ask them to write down something that God has impressed upon
them during the service, about how they'll be different. They can
pin it up in a prominent place or put in a wallet, purse or pocket to
find later in the week.

Meditation: it's in the post!

Lord, see these hands?
they want to be busy and creative for you,
writing, making, mending, selling
daily works of art, packages of beauty,
surprising others, created with care.
Lord, see these feet?
they want to be postmen of good news,
walking with purpose, running to someone's side,
bringing help, serving others with joy.
Lord, see this smile?
It's a postcard from you to others around us,
that tells them we love being part of your company,
working beside you to make our world great.

Closing prayer

Lord Jesus Christ,
You worked here on earth
and learnt from people around you,
help us, as we go from here,
to work and learn to your glory.
Grant us wisdom to make good decisions,
and the courage to do what is right.
Give us strength when we are weary,
and peace when we are stressed.
Anoint our creativity and energy, so that even our smallest tasks
honour you.
Above all, help us to bring your presence into our work or school.
Amen

Display: where's the church on Monday morning ?

Tell people that at the end of the service you would like them all
to write or draw something on a large sheet of paper which shows
what they do on a Monday morning. Then they sign it. This could
be done earlier in the service if there's time, or if you'd prefer.

MEMO

Date:

To:

From:

Re:

'I am the Lord your God.
I am holding your hand,
so don't be afraid.
I am here to help you.'
Isaiah 41.13

Might come in handy

About slaves

Slavery was taken for granted in the ancient world. At its worst, slavery was a life of brutally hard work. But at its best, a slave might be treated as virtually a member of the family – more akin to an employee or servant.

Slaves could gain their freedom in a number of ways (Ex. 21.2–27; Lev. 25.47–55; Deut. 15.12–23). Relatives or friends could buy them out of service, or the owner might set the slave free. On their release, it was expected that the slave would be given a 'leaving gift' of money. They would also take their master's name.

Within Roman society, slaves could not legally marry, nor could they own any property in their own name. They could be harshly treated and unjustly punished; but they could also be very well treated and even given lots of responsibility. Many slaves, for example, ran their master's business; others were highly skilled family retainers. (For example, many doctors were slaves – sort of like the family physician – and it is entirely possible that Luke was an ex-slave who had taken his master's name of Lucius.)

Against such a background, it is not really surprising that Paul and other New Testament writers did not call for the abolition of slavery: it probably would have been unthinkable that such a change was possible. However, that should not blind us to the extremely radical nature of Paul's writing. He argued that slaves should be treated with respect (Titus 2.9; Col. 3.22; 4.1) and he even made the astonishing claim that in Christ there was no real difference between slave and free (1 Cor. 12.13).

Getting ready

A week (or more) before

PairTalk: where are you on Monday morning?

☐ Put questions on Powerpoint

Game: what's my line?

☐ Select and brief your 'mystery guests'

Gordon's Monday morning blues

☐ Photocopy script

TakeAway: a memo to yourself

☐ Photocopy memo format

Display: where's the church on Monday morning?

☐ Get large piece of paper/card for people to write on

An hour (or more) before

☐ Arrange seating and set

Gordon's Monday morning blues

☐ Set-up for Gordon (microphone, statue, etc. as required)

TakeAway: a memo to yourself

☐ Put memos in place

Family

Born to shop

8. BORN TO SHOP

Aim: To view and use money in God's way

Bible: Matthew 6.19–20; 7.11

1. Want it!

The purpose here is to
- acknowledge what God gives us
- get people to think about what gifts they'd like

We do this by asking people to
- listen to a description of God
- talk in pairs and feed back to group
- listen to Gordon and the story

The tools we use are
- Stand up and listen: God the giver
- PairTalk: all I want for Christmas
- Drama: Gordon's answerphone
- Story: Richard Phule part 1

2. Watch it!

The purpose here is to
- find out what the Bible says about wealth and possessions

We do this by asking people to
- look up Bible verses
- pray
- listen to story and to Gordon
- answer Gordon's questions

The tools we use are
- Bible: Matthew 6.19–20; 7.11
- Prayer: change our hearts
- Story: Richard Phule part 2
- Drama: Gordon's back
- Game: searching for the pearls

3. Try it!

The purpose here is to
- help people to strip away the excess materialism from Christmas celebrations

We do this by asking people to
- think about Christmas materialism
- suggest alternative ways of giving

The tools we use are
- Comment: the modern Christmas
- The Alternative Alternative Gift Catalogue

4. Live it!

The purpose here is to
- help people to celebrate Christmas simply

We do this by asking people to
- pray
- listen to the story
- take away gift vouchers

The tools we use are
- Story: Richard Phule part 3
- TakeAway: gift vouchers
- Prayer: shopping prayer
- Closing prayer

Running order

When	What	Who
	Want it!	
	Welcome: born to shop?	
	Stand up and listen: God the giver	
	PairTalk: all I want for Christmas	
	Drama: Gordon's answerphone	
	Story: Richard Phule part 1	
	Watch it!	
	Bible: Matthew 6.19–20; 7.11	
	Prayer: change our hearts	
	Story: Richard Phule part 2	
	Drama: Gordon's back	
	Game: searching for the pearls	
	Try it!	
	Comment: the modern Christmas	
	The Alternative Alternative Gift Catalogue	
	Live it!	
	Story: Richard Phule part 3	
	TakeAway: Alternative gift vouchers	
	Prayer: shopping prayer	
	Closing prayer	

Want it!

Welcome: born to shop?

LEADER: Today we'll be looking at the need to have and the need to give. Are we born to shop – or too bored to shop?

Stand up and listen: God the giver

Stand up everybody and listen:
listen to what our God is like.
He is our king and our lord,
and our father too.
He knows how to give us good gifts,
and is ready when people ask.[1]
He give us the earth, and all that is in it,
food day by day, forgiveness, too.[2]
He gives us orders –
orders that make sense –
to love one another, as he has loved us.[3]
He has given us his Son,
Jesus – God with us –
a man we can look at and see what God is like;
a man we can look at and
know what it means to be
made in the image of God.[4]
He has given us grace and flair
for different types of service
so we can work for others
with joy in our hearts.[5]
And that's not all. If we ask,
there is so much he will give us:
the Holy Spirit, and a new heart, too;
justice, and strength in time of need;
victory and joy,
freedom and peace,
life – everlasting life.
God graciously gives us all these things:
Things that will last forever.[6]

---

[1] *Matt. 7.11;* [2] *Matt. 6.9;* [3] *John 13.34;* [4] *Col. 1.15;* [5] *1 Pet. 4.10;*
[6] *Rom. 2.7;*

PairTalk: all I want for Christmas

LEADER: How do we know it's nearly Christmas? Because we've started thinking about giving and receiving presents already! Is that what it's all about? No, but as usual, we humans don't miss a trick and can't bear to pass up the opportunity for another spending spree.

> ▷ What do you want for your next birthday or Christmas present?
> ▷ Why do you think you want it?

People can chat about it or draw answers on paper.

If done at Christmas, the paper can be in the shape of a Christmas decoration and can be hung on a Xmas tree.

Get feedback, show pictures.

For each 'want', talk about why the person wants it.

LEADER: But do belongings do the trick? Do they deliver on what they promise? A few days after Christmas, how important are they? There are many different reasons why we might want certain things. We might want something because it's really useful, or because we'll really enjoy it. Sometimes, if we're honest, we want things because we've seen them on adverts, or because everyone else has got one. Let's ask Gordon for his perspective.

Gordon's answerphone

This can be pre-recorded, or acted live.

GORDON: *(Recording)* Hello, I'm afraid Gordon the Gargoyle isn't available to answer the phone right now. I've gone out shopping, 'cos now all the shops are open on Sunday, it's great. You can shop seven days a week!

What's more, I've left a replica gargoyle in my place so no-one will even notice I've gone! If you'd like to leave a message, please do so after the tone. Otherwise, try ringing me after six o'clock tonight, by which time I will probably have run out of money.

LEADER: Well, that's no help. He's just as bad as us. Let's have a story instead.

Story: Richard Phule part 1

NARRATOR: Once upon a time there was a boy called Richard. Richard Phule (that's spelt P-H-U-L-E as he was always explaining to people.)

The Phule family were big in turnips. In fact, Richard's father had cornered the market in turnips for many years and his turnip processing plant employed many thousands of people.

Many of these came from Richard's own family.

Richard had a big family. Along with his parents and grandparents he had seven aunts and seven uncles. And then he had twenty five cousins and thirty seven first cousins. And a second cousin twice removed called Boris. Nobody seemed to know much about Boris.

Having a big family made Richard very happy. Not because he liked his family, but because he got lots of presents on his birthday and at Christmas. Richard loved getting presents. And quite often, something happened which he loved even more. His parents, grandparents, seven aunts, seven uncles, twenty five cousins, thirty seven first cousins and a second cousin twice removed called Boris couldn't think what to get him so they sent money instead.

One Christmas, Richard's father took him Christmas shopping. They went to the biggest toyshop in the town. Richard was amazed! He had never seen so many toys.

'I want that,' he said to his father, pointing to a large games console with a 42-inch screen hi-fi speakers and a built-in toaster.

'But Richard,' explained his father, 'We're supposed to be buying presents for other people.'

'Other people?' spluttered Richard. 'I don't care about other people! What's the point of wasting my money on other people?'

'But that's what happens at Christmas,' said his father, wondering if he could take his son into Santa's grotto and just leave him there.

'Well, they can all have a tube of Smarties,' said Richard. 'Everyone likes Smarties.'

'But...' said his father.

'Please, father,' said Richard, 'It's for their own good. After all, we don't want them to be spoiled do we?'

So Richard bought 81 tubes of Smarties. That's one each for his parents, grandparents, seven aunts, seven uncles, twenty five cousins, thirty seven first cousins. He didn't bother buying a present for his second cousin twice removed called Boris on account of how no-one seemed to know where he lived. Having done his Christmas shopping, Richard then went and bought a lot of toys ... for himself.

As they neared home, Richard noticed that someone was sitting outside the gates of his father's house. It was a beggar, sitting there in rags. He was wearing an odd pair of shoes and an old army greatcoat tied around his waist with a piece of string.

'Spare any change, guv?' said the beggar.

'Of course,' replied Richard's father and he gave the beggar a five pound note. Richard couldn't believe his eyes.

'What are you doing, father?' he demanded.

'Well, this poor man has no money,' explained his father.

'Oh per-lease,' said Richard. 'Have you no grasp of modern macro-economics? You can't invest in failing businesses. This man is a sponger, a parasite, a leech on society. You're only encouraging him.'

'I don't care,' said his father. He took a long hard look at Richard. 'Sometimes I wonder if there wasn't a slip-up at the hospital,' he muttered.

'Anyway, I think we should take the money back,' said Richard. But when they turned to speak to the beggar, there was no-one there. He had seemingly disappeared.

'Now, where on earth did he go?' enquired Richard's father.

'Oh, who cares?' replied Richard testily. 'Let's just get indoors. It's starting to snow.'

On Christmas Day, Richard went downstairs to start work on his presents. His parents gave him a new, gold wristwatch. Cousin Boris even sent him a pair of binoculars. Richard was just trying these out, looking out of the window, when he thought he saw the beggar again. But he wasn't sitting outside this time; he was standing in the street, staring at Richard. When Richard looked again, he was gone.

It gave Richard an uncomfortable feeling. But he put it down to the three boxes of After Eight mints he had eaten for breakfast, and he soon turned and carried on with his presents.

Watch it!

Bible: Matthew 6.19–21; 7.11

LEADER: We've seen what Richard thinks about money. But what does the Bible say? This is what Jesus said in his Sermon on the Mount.

Read Matthew 6.19–21

LEADER: Out of all those things you listed that you want for Christmas, how many of them will last? How many of them will be of lasting value?

The things we see around us – in the shops, on the internet, in the adverts on TV, seem so appealing. But, as Jesus says, will they just rust and moulder away (Mt. 6.19)?

Jesus challenges you to think about where your heart is – I don't mean the heart that's pumping the blood round your body all the time. We know where that is.

I mean the very centre of your being. The essential you. The 'you' that would still be there, even if your body changed completely, or were taken away. Instead of accumulating treasure on earth – storing up money and possessions around us – he challenges us to think long-term: to put God and his kingdom first. Because that's the only thing that's going to last.

But it's very difficult to change the direction of your heart. Perhaps the only thing that can change us is prayer. Talking to God changes us. His Spirit gets going inside us and we begin to change, we become like God. And our hearts begin to want different things.

One of the things we want is to see the kingdom of God here on earth. Jesus' prayer was, 'Your kingdom come, your will be done, on earth, as it is in heaven.' God's interested in giving us really good gifts, at Christmas, and throughout our lives.

Read Matthew 7.11.

Prayer: change our hearts

Lord, when we look in shop windows, or at adverts, or on the internet,
everything looks so appealing and we want it all now.
Help us to remember which things are most important,
and to hear your words ringing in our ears.
Help us to think about the effect of wanting so much.
Only you can change our hearts.
Make us into people who obey you first
and so who are always generous.
Amen

Story: Richard Phule part 2

LEADER: Do you remember Richard Phule? He didn't really like giving to the
beggar. Let's see what he's up to now.

It's twenty years later, and a lot has changed...

NARRATOR: By the time he was forty, Richard was head of his own business.

Of course, it hadn't *always* been his own business. Originally, it was his
father's firm, National Turnips, which Richard had taken over as the result
of a boardroom coup.

Some people questioned the ruthless way in which Richard had man-
aged to become Chairman of the Board and then sacked his own father.
But anyone who did question it was also sacked by Richard as well, so
very soon everyone stopped asking questions and settled down to doing
as they were told.

So, when Richard renamed the company Turnips'R'Us in an attempt to
appeal to the American market, and when he introduced some ruthless
cost-cutting measures, including sacking most of the remaining family
members, no-one dared object.

You might think that Richard should have behaved better towards his
father. Not to mention his seven aunts, seven uncles, twenty five cousins,
thirty seven first cousins and his second cousin twice removed called
Boris. But Richard had no time for all that. He knew that business was not
about emotion. It was about the figures; about making profit.

So he was a bit surprised when, at first, he felt uncomfortable talking to
his father. Every time they talked he felt strange, like there was something
wrong. In the end, he felt so uncomfortable that he stopped talking to
his father at all.

He never went to see his father any more, and never returned his phone
calls. The uncomfortable feeling went away and gradually, as the years
went by, Richard convinced himself that he'd done the right thing.

One day, Richard did something that he had never done before: he went
to church. He didn't want to go to church, of course, but this was a bit of
business. Richard had noticed that the church was appealing for money
for repairs, and he spotted a chance for a bit of promotion.

The Vicar was explaining why the money was needed.

' First, we need to repair the roof, fix the font, prop up the pulpit, and change the chancel,' he said. 'Then we need to lower the lectern, shore up the steeple and patch up the porch. Finally, we need to blow up the entire PCC.'

'I'm sorry?' said Richard.

'Oh, no. Forget the last one,' said the vicar. 'Just daydreaming, that's all.'

'Well, I'll be happy to help you,' said Richard. 'I'll give you money to do all those things. But you have to do something for me in return.'

'And what would that be?' asked the vicar.

'Oh, nothing very much,' replied Richard. 'Just rename the church.'

'Rename the church?' The vicar had gone a funny colour. (Actually, he was quite a funny colour to start with, but now he'd gone an entirely *different*, funny colour.)

'I couldn't help noticing that this building is named after some bloke no-one's ever heard of,' said Richard.

'St Paul,' said the vicar.

'Exactly. So all you have to do is rename it the Church of Richard Phule. That's spelt P-h-u-l-e,' he explained quickly.

'But I couldn't do that,' said the vicar.

'Why on earth not?' asked Richard. 'After all, if I'm giving you all this dosh, I want people to know who's behind it.'

'Couldn't you give the money anonymously?' asked the vicar.

'Don't be daft,' said Richard. 'What's the point of giving anonymously? How would anyone know you'd given it? You want to let everyone know how generous you are.'

At that point their conversation was interrupted.

An old woman was shuffling her way across the back of the church to where a small metal box was fixed in the wall. She took an absolute age to get there, and when she had she took out her purse, incredibly slowly, and carefully selected a tiny coin. She put the coin in the box and then turned and slowly made her way out again.

'And she'll have to go as well,' said Richard. 'I mean, that's your problem isn't it? What kind of investor is that?' said Richard. 'You'll never get any-where if you have people who only give you 5p.'

'That's as may be,' said the vicar. 'But I know that old lady. She hasn't got two beans to rub together but she gives as much as she can afford. With-out anyone seeing her. You could afford to buy this church a thousand times over. Yet you want everyone to know it's you. Thank you for your offer, but I'm afraid we'll look elsewhere for the money.'

And he turned and walked away.

'That's the problem with the church today,' said Richard. 'No business sense at all.'

But he couldn't help noticing that the strange 'uncomfortable' feeling had returned.

Drama: Gordon's back

LEADER: We're going to leave the story there for a bit...

GORDON: Excuse me!

LEADER: Who's that? Gordon? Are you back from your shopping?

GORDON: Yes, and you know what? I agree with a lot of what that nice Richard man says. What's the point of buying people presents, when you could spend the money on yourself?

LEADER: Gordon! That's not very generous!

GORDON: Well, I'm not feeling generous. Every year I buy all my friends presents and I get a load of rubbish back. Last year, I bought Glenda a lovely scarf, because she was complaining of the draughts. And you know what she gave me? A DVD.

LEADER: Well, that sounds OK.

GORDON: A DVD which she got free with the newspaper: *The Happy World of Eastenders*.

LEADER: Well, at least it was short. But Gordon, maybe there's a reason why she gave you that. Maybe she hasn't got much money or something like that.

GORDON: That is not the point. Even if you haven't got much money you should still spend a lot. That's why they invented credit cards. So this year, I've decided only to give to people who I know are going to give me something decent in return. That's the spirit of Christmas.

LEADER: I'm sure that's not right.

 ▷ What would you say to Gordon?

LEADER: You see? Other people here don't think you're right.

GORDON: I don't care. I want to get something out of Christmas for myself.

LEADER: Do you think that's how God views it? Do you think that's God's way of giving — only giving if he's going to get something back?

GORDON: I don't care. I'm off now to watch my *Eastenders* DVD and cheer myself up.

LEADER: Well, let's hope that Gordon listens to the rest of the service. He might change his mind. Because here are some things that Jesus did say about giving:

Game: searching for the pearls

Hide a number of wrapped presents around the church. How many is up to you and will depend on the number of children in your church. Some could look very large and flash, others small and insignificant, maybe wrapped with newspaper or brown paper.

Only three contain Bible verses. These are the pearls.

▷ *Matthew 10.8 Freely you have received, freely give.*

▷ *Luke 6.38 Give and it will be given to you.*

▷ *Acts 20.35 It is more blessed to give than receive.*

The children (or adults) who find these three get a prize.

LEADER: Now, how do we put all that into practice? Let's think about what we do at Christmas, for example.

Try it!

Comment: the modern Christmas

LEADER: Christmas celebrations, as we know them today, have a relatively short history. Whilst in the UK Christmas has been a customary holiday for hundreds of years, in America, Christmas wasn't an official holiday until 1870. Looking further back, the church didn't even mark the birthday of Christ until the fourth century. But now it's the biggie. And mainly that's down to money.

Of course, people have always spent money at public holidays. In the past, this was mainly spent on food and drink. But over the course of the nineteenth century, merchants and traders discovered that you could sell other things as well. New Year's Day was among the first to be used in this way. In the first half of the nineteenth century, New Year's Day presents were as popular as Christmas presents, with St Valentine's Day not far behind.

But Christmas soon emerged as the clear winner. And by the turn of the twentieth century, the commercial promotion of Christmas was everywhere.

Today, it has grown enormously. Many businesses rely on Christmas for their survival. Woolworths, for example, makes around two-thirds of its sales in the run-up to the festive season.

But for many people, the idea of a Christmas season that starts somewhere around the end of September seems a little bit over the top. Increasingly they are looking for alternatives.

The Alternative Alternative Gift Catalogue

Hold up an alternative gift catalogue – such as that issued by World Vision.

LEADER: These catalogues have really taken off in the past few years.

They offer alternative gifts – gifts that actually go to someone else. So, instead of buying someone a present, you buy something for a community in the developing world, on their behalf.

? ▷ How many people have used this? What did you buy?

LEADER: I wonder if there aren't other alternatives we could add to our own catalogue.

Get as big a sheet of paper as you can – maybe you can use wallpaper joined together. It needs to be visible. When ideas come back from the groups write them up on the huge sheet – it will become your church's Alternative Alternative Gift Catalogue.

You can find more ideas for alternative gifts in the 'Might Come in Handy' section (p.123). These could be put onto PowerPoint or introduced after the discussion, if they haven't been thought of already.

What alternative gifts could we give each other?

Maybe this year we could set ourselves the target of only spending £1 on each gift.

Maybe our gift to someone else is something we wish for them. You could start by drawing it. Perhaps they need refreshing – you could draw a cup of tea, a long bath, an evening to themselves.

Maybe we should ignore money and things completely and think about time or services we can offer.

Think about some kindness to offer them: time to meet for a chat, time to unwind, time away from the children, help with household or garden jobs.

Think about what you've got: skills, possessions you can share, time.

Maybe it's something that you can make.

Decide what you could offer that requires no purchase, simply your offer of time and sharing.

 ▷ What alternative gift ideas can you suggest?

Get feedback from the groups and write the different ideas onto the big Alternative Gift Catalogue at the front.

Then get people individually to start thinking about what, if any, of these gifts they would choose for each other.

Live it!

Story: Richard Phule part 3

NARRATOR: It was Christmas Eve.

Turnips'R'Us had grown steadily over the years and had now become PHULE INC. (That's P-H-U-L-E I-N-C) a multi-national conglomerate with outlets in Australia, America, Argentina, Austria, Andorra and Chipping Sodbury. Turnips were the food of the moment. Richard had leveraged the turnip market and expanded fast; you could now get Turnip Ice Cream and Turnip Yoghurt. You could buy Turnip a la Greque, Turnip Niçoise and Turnip Chipping Sodbury. You could enjoy Turnip Mousse, Turnip Paté and the best-selling spread, I Can't Believe it's Not Turnip.

But Richard was not a happy man. He had married twice, but neither of these marriages had lasted, victims of his relentless drive for the most profitable turnip. He knew that no-one really liked him. He was the boss, he didn't expect to be liked. But he felt lonely sometimes. That old, uncomfortable feeling had never quite gone away.

Sometimes he thought about his family; about his parents and grandparents, his seven aunts, seven uncles, twenty five cousins, thirty seven first cousins and second cousin twice removed called Boris. He wondered what they were doing now. He thought occasionally of phoning his father and talking to him, but he didn't know the number and, anyway, he had no idea where the old man was living now.

So it was, that six o'clock in the evening, on Christmas Eve, the international Offices of Phule Inc. were deserted. Everyone had gone to their homes and families to start celebrating Christmas. Everyone except Richard.

'Never mind,' he thought to himself. 'I'll go and have a drink.' So he went out, said goodnight to the security guard, and crossed the road to get some money out at a cash machine.

He put in his card and typed in his number.

The words, 'I'm sorry, your account has been closed' came up on the screen. And the plastic card came out again.

'Closed?' muttered Richard. 'Closed?'

He put his card in and tried again.

The machine gave a whirring noise.

'Look,' it flashed onto the screen. 'I'm a very busy ATM. I told you the first time. The account has been closed. Now leave me alone. It's Christmas Eve, you know.' Once more the card was ejected.

Now Richard was angry. He rammed his card in and punched in the numbers.

A message came up on the screen.

'OK,' it read, 'Do I have to spell it out? You have no money. It's all gone. The bank has closed your account. It's not my problem.' It paused. 'Press "Enter" if you require any further abuse.'

Richard spent the next hour feverishly making telephone calls. Or rather, he spent the next fifty seven minutes making telephone calls, because he was half way through talking to his accountant when the mobile phone company cut him off.

It was true. His business had collapsed. There had been an international plunge in the turnip market. The Far East had developed a new super-parsnip which had completely undercut the turnip trade.

Not only that, but a report on *Panorama* revealed that eating I Can't Believe it's Not Turnip led to hair loss, itching and double vision. In just a few short hours shares in Phule Inc. had collapsed. Richard had lost everything he owned. His bank manager told him that his house had been repossessed, his car taken back and his cat had been sold on eBay.

'But how can this have happened?' moaned Richard.

'Clearly you have no grasp of macro-economics,' replied the bank manager. 'Now if you don't mind I've got to go. It's Christmas Eve, you know.'

And then he hung up.

So that was it. It was now late on Christmas Eve. Richard had no money and nowhere to live. He had no-one to turn to.

He would have to get the money from somewhere. 'I know,' he thought, 'I'll sell my wristwatch. It must be worth something.' Yet something in him hated the idea. The watch had been a present from his father; it represented Richard's last link with his family. But there was no choice.

Just round the corner there was an antiques shop. In spite of the fact that the shop was closed, he hammered on the door until a figure appeared in the darkness.

'What do you want?' asked the shopkeeper from the other side of the door.

'I need to sell my watch,' said Richard.

'I'm very sorry, but we're closed,' replied the shopkeeper. 'It's Christmas Eve, you know.'

'I KNOW IT'S CHRISTMAS EVE!' shouted Richard. 'EVERYONE KEEPS TELLING ME THAT. I'VE EVEN HAD A FLIPPING MACHINE TELLING ME THAT. I KNOW IT'S CHRISTMAS EVE BUT I'VE GOT NOTHING LEFT AND NOWHERE TO GO AND YOU'RE MY ONLY HOPE!' He trailed off. Desperately Richard searched for the word to change the shopkeeper's mind. 'Please,' he said, using a word he hadn't used in years. 'Please...'

The shopkeeper turned, thought for a moment, then opened the door.

'All right,' he said. 'Just this once.'

It was very dark in the shop as Richard entered.

'Hang on,' said the shopkeeper. 'Let me turn on a few more lights.'

Richard took off his hat and laid it on the counter. He felt very miserable and lonely.

'I've got to sell my watch,' He explained without looking around. 'My business has collapsed and I've no-one to turn to. I just need enough money to find somewhere to stay.'

A solitary tear ran down his nose and splashed on to the counter. 'I wish I could start again,' he said. 'I wish I could change things. Maybe then I wouldn't be here now.' He wiped his nose on his sleeve. He would have used his handkerchief but it had all been repossessed by the people who did his laundry.

'I'm sorry,' he said. 'Just tell me what the watch is worth and I'll go.'

Suddenly, he realised that the shopkeeper was looking at him.

'I wouldn't dream of buying this watch,' said the shopkeeper. 'I gave it to you thirty-five years ago and I'm not taking it back.'

Suddenly Richard realised who the figure was. 'Second Cousin Twice Removed Boris!' he shouted.

'No!' replied the shopkeeper. 'I'm your father! Boris gave you the binoculars, you fool.'

'Father?' said Richard. It was his own father, the father he never thought to see again.

'Come and stay here,' said his father. 'We'll have Christmas together.'

'But why would you want me?' asked Richard. 'I took everything you had. I never returned your calls. I treated you so badly.'

'But now you're back,' said his father. 'I've always loved you, Richard, even when you didn't love me. And I've been here waiting.'

'And you'll take me back?'

'Of course,' replied his father. 'It's Christmas. Everybody takes things back at Christmas.'

Richard smiled. 'I don't have a gift for you, I'm afraid,' he said.

His father laughed.

'Yes, you do,' he said. 'You've come home. That's the only gift I ever wanted.'

And that Christmas Richard went and celebrated with his family; with his parents and grandparents, his seven aunts and seven uncles, his twenty five cousins and thirty seven first cousins.

And, of course, his second cousin twice removed called Boris.

TakeAway: alternative gift vouchers

People can now make their own gift vouchers. (Or they can take away one to use as a template and design or photocopy their own. Alternatively, you could offer to email the vouchers in an attachment to people in your church who are interested.)

They can then write in these vouchers something they are going to do/make/give to someone, based on the ideas generated during the Alternative Alternative Gift Catalogue session.

Prayer: shopping prayer

Be with us, Lord, when we go shopping.

If we have very little money, help us to choose wisely and not to grumble about things we can't afford.

Make us content, in spite of all the voices and pictures around us, inviting us to spend all we've got.

If we have plenty of money, save us from spending it all on ourselves so that we can give generously to those who are in need.

Help us never to value our possessions more than people, but to be ready to share them cheerfully with others.

Lord, guard our hearts, that we may treasure you above all else and so store up treasure in heaven.

Amen

Closing prayer

We are deeply grateful, Lord,
for the treasure we possess,
for the people who love us,
for the comfort in our lives.
And we are asked to share this gold,
which we gladly do;
it is not ours to keep.
But there is more.
You have placed deep within, buried treasure in our hearts:
hopes, dreams, desires, dissatisfactions,
a sense of sorrow and a sense of humour,
which, when unlocked, can bring us close to you.
We share this too:
exchange the matchwood of our lives for the glitter of your grace.
For the baby strewn in straw is now the pearl-gem of great price.
Amen

Might come in handy

Ideas for alternative vouchers

▷ a morning or evening's babysitting
▷ mending things
▷ an artycrafty session for kids
▷ taking children out
▷ an hour's ironing
▷ a week/month of early morning cups of tea
▷ a gardening job
▷ organising a birthday party
▷ a Sunday lunch or an evening meal
▷ a poem or story
▷ a painting
▷ a meal or a cake

About Christmas presents

The origin of the Christmas present seems to have a number of different sources. The earliest references to presents being given on or around the winter solstice comes from Ancient Rome during the feast of Kalends. Then, high ranking officials were expected to give gifts to the Emperor.

The feast-day of St Nicholas, who was remembered for his charitable giving, was also occasionally marked by gift-giving. Parents might leave small gifts of sweetmeats or fruit for their children.

But those are isolated examples. Gift-giving in the modern sense starts in the 1820s, when the practice of exchanging small gifts blossomed – or is that mutated? – into the full-on gift-fest we now know.

Complaints about Christmas have been happening ever since. Harriet Beecher Stowe wrote a story in the 1850s where a character complains how when she was a child, 'the very idea of a present was new!' and that 'there are worlds of money wasted at this time of year.'

Getting ready

A week (or more) before

PairTalk: all I want for Christmas

☐ Put questions on Powerpoint

Drama: Gordon's answerphone/ Gordon's back

☐ Photocopy script. Record message if possible.

Story: Richard Phule

☐ Copy script.

☐ Find comfy story chair and a good story teller!

Game: searching for the pearls

☐ Find boxes and put verses into three of them

☐ Wrap up boxes as Christmas presents

Alternative Alternative Gift Catalogue

☐ Put suggestions on Powerpoint if necessary

TakeAway: alternative gift vouchers

☐ Photocopy voucher format

An hour (or more) before

☐ Arrange seating and set

Drama: Gordon's answerphone/ Gordon's back

☐ Set-up for Gordon (microphone, statue, etc. as required)

Game: searching for the pearls

☐ Hide boxes around church

TakeAway: alternative gift vouchers

☐ Put vouchers in place

Appendix
Introducing Gordon the Gargoyle

To be used the first time we meet Gordon.

LEADER: I'd like to introduce you to someone who's going to help out with these services. He's called Gordon. And he's a gargoyle. Hello? Hello? Gordon? Are you there?

GORDON: Of course I'm here. I'm always here.

Leader asks children if they can see where Gordon is. Get the little ones to say 'Hello' to him.

LEADER: So what are you Gordon?

GORDON: I'm a gargoyle.

LEADER: What's that?

GORDON: Well, it's kind of a statue. I'm considered decorative.

LEADER: Are you? Why? And how long have you been going to church?

GORDON: Six hundred years.

LEADER: Six hundred years!

GORDON: Well, when you're made of stone, time isn't the same. I'm considered a sprightly young thing. Graham Gargoyle over there is nine hundred years old.

LEADER: Anyway, it's nice to hear from you...

Then into rest of sketch.

The Gargoyle himself.